The Story of Boxes

The Good, The Bad & The Ugly

The Secret to Human Liberation, Peace and Happiness

By Rúna Magnúsdóttir & Nicholas Haines

Praise for
The Story of Boxes,
the Good, the Bad and the Ugly

"Imagine a world where people were not judged based on their outer appearance, where each of us felt comfortable and were encouraged to be our true selves at all times. In such a world we would have the freedom to live, love and share ourselves with others from the heart and soul with confidence. *The Story of Boxes* offers an eye-opening perspective on how we can create such a world.

Rúna and Nick have written a brilliant treatise on the life-stifling, human-potential-limiting and dream-thwarting effects of bias, prejudice and socially-coerced conformity. Having escaped from a few boxes which held me back from expressing my Authentic Self and drove me to make career choices which were depressing I appreciate what this book can do for others. By exploring the natural human inclination to categorize and box people in the reader gains the insight, compassion and courage needed to liberate themselves and others from the boxes which do not serve them. Our education system would do well to incorporate the #NoMoreBoxes Movement into their culture and curricula."

~ Andrea Pennington, MD Author of "I Love You, Me!" and
Co-Founder of the #RealSelfLove Movement
www.RealSelf.love

"The concept that we place ourselves and others into boxes is startling obvious and yet hidden in plain sight. As someone that has worked throughout my life towards positive personal and social transformation to accelerate the pace of individual and collective awakening, I think this book is essential reading for everyone, especially our children."

~ Chris Attwood, Co-author of the New York Times Best
Sellers, The Passion Test and Your Hidden Riches

"As a businesswoman and someone who has spent years in both in the private and public sector, I recognize that creating change that is inclusive and sustainable can be difficult. Once I read the Story of Boxes I knew that it contained many solutions that are both simple to grasp and deeply profound in their actions."

~ Thordis Loa Thorhallsdottir,
Deputy Mayor Reykjavik, Iceland

"My belief is that we can change the course of history and become a truly sustainable planet. The Story of Boxes highlights the very best and worst of what it is to be human. It offers a simple way forward to develop a more inclusive society. By making pertinent changes in our lives, we will positively transform the world in which we live."

~ Molly Bedingfield, Founder & CEO of
Global Angel Foundation

Contents

Introduction

Ever heard someone say something like, "Men are like this," or "Women are like that" - or, perhaps more recently, "Millennials think this way"?

If so, you were witnessing a cognitive "box" in the making.

"Boxes" are used here as a metaphor for a specific mode of thinking that's embedded in virtually all of humanity: a mode of thinking that's based on grouping, classifying, and categorizing people, things, and ideas.

Boxes, however, are not accurate representations of reality; they are fiction - a mental fantasy of sorts, but one that seems so believable.

What if, for example, you're a woman, and — despite typical ideas of what a woman is supposed to be like - your leadership style isn't really focused on collaboration? Or what if you're a man, and instead of adopting a leadership approach that's domineering or assertive, you prefer to lead with compassion and collaboration?

Or, perhaps, you're a millennial - and you actually don't live your life through your phone?

The list goes on and on, of course. Putting people in boxes limits all of us and places walls around who we are and what we can become.

The Birth of the #NoMoreBoxes Movement

In March 2018, Rúna and Nick, along with The Change Makers (a group of international thought leaders and business experts), were invited to the Impact Leadership

Global Summit 2018, which was held at the United Nations Headquarters. Sitting on various panel discussions, they were there to help address some of the most pressing issues facing humanity, helping the world move forward with realising the UN's 17 Sustainable Development Goals.

In one panel, "Conversations with Men", where the subject of gender equality was raised, Nick highlighted a stunning reality: the world is very slow in moving towards true gender equality. The reason for this, the towering obstacle in the way of greater equality, comes down to all the limiting boxes that we, as humans, are putting each other into.

In his talk, Nick noted how we've put many of the softer skills in the "feminine" box - and the more assertive, power-based traits and behaviours in a "masculine" box.

The result?

A man who is brilliant at soft skills is often deemed feminine - perhaps labelled "soft" and told to "man up." A woman who is ambitious, powerful and driven is viewed as too masculine. She is told not to be so butch but to be more "ladylike" and feminine. Because her behaviour doesn't match the box that has been assigned to her female gender, she is harshly criticised.

Neither of these worlds of judgement work. In fact, these judgements say much more about those who judge. As Rúna listened to Nick explain the simple elegance of "boxes", and how they touch our lives in so many ways, she finally got the answer to a question she'd been asking herself for a long time: *"What really needs to happen to make our shared existence more equal and fair and just?"*

The answer struck her right then and there (at none other than the UN Headquarters): we need to empower humans with the tools and knowledge to become more aware of their own boxes; their limiting beliefs and habits.

The Traffic Jam

The next day, the news of The Change Makers speaking at the United Nations was eclipsed by dire warnings about an imminent snowstorm that was about to hit the East Coast of the United States. Many flights were cancelled - even flights that were scheduled several days later. New York was locking down in the face of a furious snow-storm.

Margareta Kull and Monique Blokzyl, two of The Change Makers, managed to get an early flight back to Sweden and Germany - their respective homes. And, later that day, Nick and Rúna took a taxi to JFK International Airport, thinking it would be a quick 40-minute journey. Two hours and 30 mins later the taxi pulled into the airport, having been stuck in a traffic jam caused by urgent preparations for the impending storm.

But what an amazing taxi ride!

You see, on this journey the whole #NoMoreBoxes movement and mission was born. Rúna and Nick enthusiastically discussed the destructive nature of boxes, the extraordinary number of boxes that we live in day in and day out, and how boxes limit all of us.

They realised how simple and accessible this idea - this metaphor - of *"boxes"* is, and how the concept of boxes opens up conversations in a light and non-judgmental way.

They explored how some boxes can be good as well as bad, how they can bring us together and tear us apart.

Finally, Nick and Rúna came to a few important questions: how do you know if you're in a box? Is there a way to start a Big Conversation about boxes - perhaps at work and in business and at home with children and family? How can we identify the boxes in our lives that serve us? And how can we identify those that don't?

That's when Rúna burst out, *"What about a Breakfast Club?! It would be a conversation that happens around a table - and with food!"* (We were probably getting hungry at that point, but regardless, food is a great conversation enabler and we went on and on)

That's how this book and the whole movement of #NoMoreBoxes (including the **#NoMoreBoxes Breakfast Club**) came to be: Nick sharing his ideas, thoughts and concerns, Rúna seeing the magic in the idea of boxes, and a very, very long taxi ride.

Embassy of Iceland in London

Exactly 6 months later to the day, we were running our very first international **#NoMoreBoxes Breakfast Club**™ at the Embassy of Iceland in London. It caused quite a stir - especially considering the high level of expertise and experience of the attending panel of delegates. Consider, for example, this one comment from one of the attendees, the inspiring **Molly Bedingfield**, President and CEO of Global Angel Foundations:

"I find the NoMoreBoxes Movement insightful and inspiring as they work to bring positive and conscious change in society. The #NoMoreBoxes Breakfast Club connected me to some fascinating people from all walks of life in a safe, non-judging atmosphere perfect for respectful and open discussion. Personally, I would love to attend another

breakfast with Nick and Rúna as facilitators - and I hope the Club springs up all over the world."

We share this same hope, too.

A Perfect Book - Full of Imperfections!

The book you're about to read has been thought about, written, rewritten, edited, and prepared for publishing in only 7 months since The Change Makers visited the UN Headquarters - and that long taxi ride. So, in a span of just 7 months, we can say without hesitation that we've created the **perfect book** - if you live in Iceland, that is.

Because if you translate the Icelandic word for "perfect" ("fullkominn") into English, the closest translation is "fully present." And we are.

We've written this book with our hearts and minds *fully present* to the problems and the joy that boxes bring to the world. We've spent months and months exploring, speaking with people and discovering our own boxes and limited ways of thinking. We've struggled, doubted our ability, and yet we've carried on writing this book *fully present* to the mission at hand.

In those conversations, deliberations, moments of self-doubt and throughout the whole process of writing this book, we have also been *fully present* to the fact that we as authors are white, European and blessed with a level of security that many people across the planet can only dream of. And as such, we only have that experience.

We don't fully know the brilliance, pride and richness of other cultures and we also don't know all the challenges, prejudice or other obstacles that other people face or experience. We only really fully know our experience. And that limits this book and fills it with imperfections.

For example, the Race Box (or whatever you'd like to call it): the box which contains all the perceptions, classifications, bigotry and prejudice related to race, countries and cultures isn't a box we feel qualified to explore based on our experience, or who we are as two white people.

We're acutely aware that we have just put ourselves in a box, but it's a box created out of respect to everyone that knows or has experienced the life outside that box in a way we will never be able to. Saying that, we don't intend to ignore that box, because, perhaps more than any box, it has led to some of the most horrific, brutal and terrible atrocities in human history and is still dividing us. So, we will write about it and highlight it but from a place of not truly knowing the prejudice and bigotry others experience.

The bottom line is, we know that this book could be *much better than what it is*. We're sure you'll find the odd mistake or typo - and perhaps our writing isn't as elegant, inclusive, styled, or even as clear as you'd like. Which we hope you'll forgive. But it is perfect - Iceland style - because we are *fully present* and care deeply about each and every human being.

This book is here to help you explore the Good, Bad, and Ugly Boxes we've created in our lives and everywhere in the world. It's a book written for you and for all of us with the best of intentions.

Do note that this book isn't here to make you feel bad or to encourage you to beat yourself up for your perceived shortcomings. Instead, on the contrary, it's meant to make you think and look at the world through a different lens - and perhaps make you smile along the way.

We want you, and all the countless other people reading this book, to use this book as a way to recognise and enjoy the boxes you love, and liberate yourself and others from the boxes that no longer serve you - or that should have never existed in the first place.

So, without further ado, welcome to this book: *The Story of Boxes, The Good, The Bad, and The Ugly.*

CHAPTER 1

BOXES ARE FOR SHOES NOT PEOPLE!

"Every human has four endowments - self awareness, conscience, independent will and creative imagination. These give us the ultimate human freedom... The power to choose, to respond, to change."

~ Stephen Covey

Have you ever felt like an outsider - like you don't fit into a setting? Or that you've been left out of a group or maybe even laughed at?

Nick knows that feeling well. One day in 1964 when he was five years old, he found himself wearing girls' underpants. Here's what happened that day, according to Nick himself.

I remember the moment so well - my mother trying to persuade me to put on my sister's dark blue school underpants. Not surprisingly, my mother was exasperated by my stubborn refusal to slip my skinny little legs into my sister's underpants and solve her laundry problem.

At the time, my mother was pregnant, probably very tired, and was trying to get her 4 children to school on time. So, I suspect that not having any boys' white underpants available was the least of her problems.

But to me? This was a big problem.

There was no way I was going to wear girls' underpants! I thought to myself. What if someone saw them? That would be rather disastrous.

Ten minutes later we were walking to school and there I was, wearing the *wrong* underpants. My mother had pointed out that gym class was tomorrow, not today, so no one would ever know my secret and I'd be okay.

I remember vividly saying goodbye to my mother at the school gates, and then one hour later hearing Mrs Jenkins say, *"We're going to have gym today and not tomorrow. So, slip down to your underpants and off we go!"*

There I was, five minutes later, standing in a sea of small skinny boys, all wearing white underpants and vests. I stood out in this crowd of boys like some sort of joke - with my bright red face and dark blue girls' underpants.

Across the room were a group of girls, wide-eyed and laughing at my appearance - much to the merriment of everyone except myself.

I was totally alone. I was crying, humiliated and horrified and I'll never forget that feeling.

Now, you may be wondering what the humiliation of a small boy in 1964 has to do with human liberation, peace, and happiness. As it turns out, this story illustrates the destructive consequences of classifying the world into certain camps or *Boxes* - whether it's classifying people, ideas, or even objects like underpants. As soon as we - individually or collectively in society - put something or someone into a box, we've created an artificial limitation for them and ourselves. And in doing so, we have increased the potential to create isolation, pain, and division.

"Boxes" are used as a metaphor for a specific mode of thinking that's embedded in virtually all of humanity: a mode of thinking that's based on grouping, classifying, and categorizing people, things, and ideas.

Now then, let's have a look at a few examples of box-based thinking so that you can catch a glimpse of how common boxes are, how deeply they infiltrate our daily lives and why they seem so believable:

For starters, picture a librarian. Then ask yourself: *What is that librarian like?*

Did you, perchance, think of someone in a wheelchair with bright pink hair? Probably not, although there are certainly plenty of librarians that either use a wheelchair or sport bright pink hair - or both. So why didn't your mind immediately conjure up a picture of a librarian with these characteristics? It's simply because (like many of us) you might have a "Librarian Box," in which you've unconsciously placed various attributes that you associate with a "librarian" - attributes which have been created based on your personal experience, popular culture, the media you consume, the beliefs you hold, and so on.

Consider a couple of other examples of boxy thinking patterns. Have you ever heard someone say something like, *"Country folk are friendlier than city dwellers,"* or *"Rich people are greedy"*?

To be sure, some people in the countryside are quite friendly, whilst some people who live in big cities keep to themselves. And yes, there are many rich people who are indeed greedy. However, there are also plenty of city inhabitants who are very friendly, and a substantial number of rich people are not at all greedy but actually very philanthropic.

The examples above illustrate that boxes are formed when our perceptions of people lump them into categories; categories like the Country Folk Box or City People Box or some other box entirely.

At this point, you may be thinking to yourself, "That's all fine and good, but I don't think like that - I don't put people into boxes. I, for one, don't assume that all rich people are greedy or that everyone in the countryside goes around with a cheery smile."

And you may not! But would you be surprised if, say, you were expecting a computer wizard to stop by your home and an 87-year-old woman knocked on your door? If so, it might be because you have a "Computer Wizard Box" (or something like that) and it doesn't have many 87-year-old women in it.

So, what's the big deal here? Why does it matter if you don't have many 87-year-old women in your Computer Wizard Box? It may not matter at all, of course, but don't be too sure: if you're a recruiter, for instance, you may unknowingly have a bias against employing an 87-year-old woman for a computer tech position precisely because such an individual doesn't fit squarely within your Computer Wizard Box. In reality, they may just be the most talented Computer Wizard in town!

Now, let's take this idea of boxes and go a little deeper by exploring a single box: the Education Box: the box which contains your collective ideas, perceptions, and classifications related to learning, students, teachers, and the like.

We've chosen to explore this box not because we consider it the most vital box to unpack or challenge, but because it's an easy box to delve into without raising too many conscious objections or unconscious resistance. That's unless you're a teacher reading this book on a Sunday afternoon, a student that's not done their homework, or someone that hates school!

And if that's the case, we apologise.

We'll begin by looking at perceptions one might hold about students. To simplify matters, we'll narrow the discussion here to university or college students. So, ponder this: what are the first 3-5 things that spring into your mind when you think of a university student?

A word of caution: to get the full benefits of this exercise, it's important that you don't try to "filter" your thoughts. Don't trick yourself by pretending that your initial thoughts were something different from what they really were. Be completely honest. When asking about the first ideas that flash into your mind when you think about a "university student" - we very literally mean the first 3-5 things that pop into your head - no matter how bizarre or shocking or unexpected they may be.

Needless to say, we have no way of knowing what ideas came to your mind just now! However, what we do know is this: when we asked other people to conduct this little exercise, they very often have quite similar initial ideas about university students. For instance, these ideas are frequently based on themes like:

University students are young, happy, and excited.

University students are lucky, ungrateful, and privileged.

University students are intense boffins.

University students drink too much and are irresponsible.

University students are having the time of their life.

University students have lots of sex and eat "junk food".

Keep in mind that we're not saying that you actually believe the first ideas that flashed into your mind when you thought about "university student". After all, your mind is constantly churning out ideas - many of which are not accurate representations of reality. What we're considering here, though, are the spontaneous, unfiltered thoughts that come to mind. Put differently, we're looking at whatever it is that you have - both good and bad and everything in between - in your University Student Box.

As implied by the title of this book - *The Story of Boxes, The Good, The Bad, and The Ugly* - here and in the following chapters you'll encounter many stories that illustrate both the power and problem of boxes. So, to that end, let's use a hypothetical story to further examine the Education Box (and its baby sister, the University Student Box) and explore some of its implications.

Suppose, for a moment, that you are 18 years old and just finishing school (of course, we recognise that the option to receive an institutionalised education is often a real privilege and one that many people do not have access to, so bear with us). Now, also suppose that all your friends were planning to go to university and that all your siblings, parents, and other relatives were university graduates. What's more, all your life you had been told, by the people in your life, that if you wanted to land a good, stable, and worthwhile job, you had to have a university education!

All of this is stewing around in your Education Box, so, quite naturally, you might feel some subtle or not-so-subtle pressure to go to university. (To be fair, such pressure might sound like a great problem to have!)

But what if you don't go to university? Will you, perhaps, grapple with the feeling that you have something to prove? Or will you experience pangs of awkwardness and uneasiness when the Education Box is opened for discussion at family gatherings? Or you'll feel proud and rebellious that you broke the mould and sledgehammered your way out of your family's Education Box?

Then again, maybe the Education Box will erode your natural instincts and compel you to go - ever so reluctantly - to college, even if it's not a good fit for you or what you want out of life. If that happens, you'll feel trapped in a life that's not your own and all because of this damned Education Box and everything you and your family have piled into it.

Now consider a very different scenario. Suppose no one in your family has gone to university and none of your friends sees a college degree in their future plans. What does your Education Box look like in this case? Maybe something like: "University just isn't for me - because people like me don't go to college."

Note that we're not saying that attending university is a good or bad thing. What we are saying, though, is that whatever is inside your Education Box can limit and trap you, as well as empower you. And therein lies one of the central paradoxes of box-based thinking: that, in extreme terms, boxes can be both very destructive and enormously useful.

You see, your boxes inform your beliefs and influence your behaviour and actions - and lead to all sorts of biases, both conscious and unconscious. Thus, boxes can very often limit your thinking and shape your beliefs about what is and what is not possible. In short, boxes can literally box you into a way of being and doing! And boxes often do this in the subtlest of ways.

For example, what if a hard-nosed business person thinks all university students are lazy, privileged toffs? That viewpoint - that box - could unconsciously influence their decision on whether or not to hire someone who happens to be a recent college grad. (And, as a matter of interest, when we brought up the "hard-nosed business person," did a man or a woman pop into your head? Welcome to the world of boxes!)

So, as you can see from these hypothetical examples, boxes are practically everywhere and profoundly influence so much of our thinking - and actions - past and present.

Your boxes inform your beliefs and influence your behaviour and actions, and lead to all sorts of biases, both conscious and unconscious.

Let's now go into a box that is both dark and terrible, before heading back briefly to the comfort of our now familiar Education Box.

We're going to open up the Race Box.

As we shared in the introduction, we are white, European and don't have firsthand experience of being anything other than that. We do however know what is right and what is wrong and how boxes can lead to the most barbaric, brutal and breathtakingly horrific examples of human behaviour. Current conservative estimates claim that over 12 million Africans were shipped across the Atlantic, as part of the transatlantic slave trade in the 16th to 19th centuries. It's also estimated that an equivalent number may have died in the procurement process.

There are many factors that led to the mass adoption of slavery, but boxes are the main reason that it was seen as normal and acceptable. Classifying one group as slaves and another as slave owners, solely based on race. Boxes at their most horrific!

We, like many people, would love to say that bad and ugly boxes based on race no longer exist. But they do, and they need to be broken down, challenged and exposed wherever they stand.

Dr Robert Pianta, Dean of the Curry School Education at the University of Virginia, explored some of the boxes that are prevalent in classroom settings, and this example shows how those boxes inform beliefs and influence behaviour and actions.

Dr Pianta and his colleagues have collected numerous video recordings of teachers presenting material and interacting with their students. By thoroughly analysing these videos, they have gained a deeper understanding of how a teacher's expectations and beliefs affect both their own behaviour as well as classroom dynamics.

Imagine, for example, that a teacher believes that boys are disruptive and require close management. This belief forms a fundamental part of that teacher's Schoolboy Box. Moreover, this belief - this way of categorizing the behaviour of schoolboys - has a very real effect on the teacher's students.

Or, as Dr Pianta puts it: *"Say I'm a teacher and I ask a question in class, and a boy jumps up and down and says, 'I know the answer! I know the answer! I know the answer!'*

"If I believe boys are disruptive and my job is to control the classroom, then I'm going to respond with, 'Johnny! You're out of line here! We need you to sit down right now.'"

Pianta explains that this sort of reaction from a teacher will probably make the boy frustrated and emotionally disengaged. The boy might then escalate his behaviour, which will, in turn, simply confirm the teacher's beliefs about him and about boys in general. Teacher and student are thus stuck in an unproductive loop.

If, however, the teacher doesn't hold these prior beliefs about schoolboys, it's unlikely that the teacher will see Johnny's behaviour as threatening. Instead, the teacher might respond with something like this, says Dr Pianta: *"'Johnny, tell me more about what you think is going on...But also, I want you to sit down quietly now as you tell that to me.'"*

"Those two responses," Dr Pianta continues, "are dictated almost entirely by two different interpretations of the same behaviour that are driven by two different sets of beliefs." (In this book, we refer to such sets of beliefs as "boxes.")

The work by Dr Pianta showcases the mighty (but largely unseen) power that boxes have on us all. When teachers placed certain children in the Schoolboy Box, based on their beliefs or what they had been told, they actually treated these children differently. As a result, the educational outcome was changed for these children - and quite possibly their entire lives.

So far in this chapter, we've highlighted the observation that all of us - just about everyone on the planet - put each other into boxes, every minute of every day. It's hardwired into us, and it's a habit that's been reinforced by millennia of social conditioning. We've considered underpants, librarians, and 87-year-old computer wizards. We've touched on the dark and terrible side of the Race Box in our history and the present day. And we've spent quite some time exploring one specific box: the Education Box, complete with hard-nosed business people, universities and disruptive boys.

As the intention of this book is to give you a sweeping introduction to the concept of box-based thinking, we think we've spent long enough in the Education Box, especially as it may not be that relevant to you.

Some of humanity's other enduring boxes include gender, race, sexuality, religion, generations and class, as well as many other attributes that lend themselves to easy classification into distinct boxes.

Although we've painted a bleak and at times horrific picture of boxes, it's important to recognise here that not all boxes are bad or destructive.

We've also created boxes that give us a sense of safety, belonging and community, as well as a sense of identity and a place to be ourselves. These may be boxes based on belonging to a church with its faith and solidarity, or a community of people that want to be identified together because of certain characteristics, interests or beliefs such as an epileptic society, transgender groups or love of a certain style of music. They are all boxes and they can have many positive qualities to them, as we shall see later.

The challenge is that a lot of boxes often have a good, bad, and perhaps an ugly side to them and they may be all mixed up together. It's not as simple as pointing to a box and declaring, "This one is good and useful," and pointing to another box and remarking imperiously, "This box is bad and wrong."

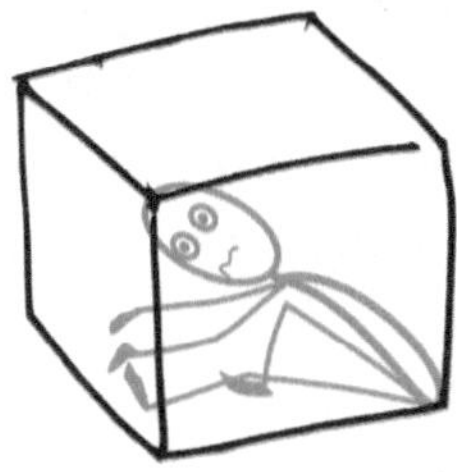

Consider the Gender Box, for example. This box has given us the joy and the strength of a sisterhood or brotherhood, as well as a place to have fun, laughter, and magical experiences, knowing we're safe and understood within that common and shared bond.

But not everything in the Gender Box is rosy. There is a dark side to this box, too, and therein lies the dilemma. The Gender Box has created the gender pay gap and inequality in the workplace and at home. It has resulted in the disgusting perception of women as sex objects, leading to the horrors of sexual exploitation and slavery and rape.

In short, the Gender Box can be a beautiful home of sharing and support and friendship. But it also leads to some of the worst atrocities we see in the world.

As you've probably guessed by the title of this book, we're going to share more about good, bad, and ugly boxes, and how to recognise them. We will show how you can liberate yourself from these boxes too. You'll even learn why all of us feel compelled to create these boxes for ourselves and others in the first place. (We think you're going to love that section - it's both fascinating and eye-opening.)

As authors, we are very similar but with one slight exception: Nick no longer wears ladies' underpants. We both abhor racism, injustice, division, and cruelty, and we hate the thought that future generations will be trapped in boxes. We long for everyone to experience a sense of liberation and the freedom to be the best versions of themselves, contributing to the world in a way that suits them, and of course to a world that is more peaceful.

This book explores the Good, Bad, and Ugly Boxes we've created in our lives and everywhere in the world. Very soon, we hope you'll spot the boxes you love and enjoy, as well as the boxes that hold you back and limit you. We also hope you'll learn to identify and work against the boxes that you know full well should be destroyed, broken and shattered into a thousand pieces.

CHAPTER 2

A LOVE AFFAIR WITH BOXES

The world is very complex and at times quite complicated, and so it makes sense to put people, behaviour, values and traits into boxes, it just doesn't make any sense for anyone to live in those boxes!

~ Nicholas Haines, Kindness Ambassador, co-creator of the #NoMoreBoxes Movement and Creator of The Vitality Test

---

You're probably reading this book because you're curious to learn and you want to grow as an individual. In which case, you may have asked yourself this question after mulling over the content so far: *"Why do we put ourselves - and others - into boxes?"*

It's a good question and one that we ourselves have thought very much about. So here, in this chapter, we will introduce you to 8 fundamental drivers that push us all towards living and operating within boxes.

The last chapter presented the whole concept of boxes - as well as some of our motivations for writing this book. It briefly explored a few of the benefits to you, and the world at large, of becoming more aware of the good, bad and ugly boxes we're all surrounded by. In this chapter, you'll learn about boxes in a bit more depth, so you can begin recognising them and decide for yourself if a particular box is worth holding onto.

You'll see us repeat this sentence a number of times: *"Awareness is the key."* There is a fundamental reason for that. (And no, it's not because we're bumbling authors and forgot that we said it before!) It's because awareness actually is the key, and we're using repetition to reinforce that idea.

If you're not aware of your boxes, nothing will change for you. Or the world. Awareness is how you can take a step back and objectively identify the boxes in your mind. It's easy to get lost in a particular box - to believe that the box is a reality, when in fact it is an illusion masquerading as reality. Thus, awareness really is the key (yes, we said it again). The key that frees your mind from the enclosing walls of boxes.

Now, with that out of the way, let's continue on with the Story of Boxes. Let's start with a bit of time travel.

Imagine that you've gone to sleep and when you wake up, you find yourself living tens of thousands of years in the past. You have a tribe to call your own, and you're living in a lush jungle or in an open, grassy plain - or even in a land of ice and snow and crisp, cool air. Wherever you are, physical survival is of the highest priority. More abstract activities, like philosophy or mathematics, are hardly of any - if any - importance here. There are far more pressing matters to consider: the weather is about to change for the worse, you need to stock up on food, and hungry predators are always lurking nearby. In short, you're living in a world where you constantly have to decide - in a matter of seconds - how to stay alive.

To survive in this environment, your brain adopts certain knowledge structures which allows you to rapidly filter out meaningless information, spot dangers, see opportunities, recognise what's new or what has changed, identify the shadowy figures on the horizon as either friendly or deadly - and to check that the children aren't playing with your new sharp stone knife.

Early on in the course of human evolution, we had to find a way to classify everything around us in a way that was efficient and quickly retrievable. We were constantly assessing information for potential danger and advantage. And thus, boxes were born.

In fact, you chose to live in your tribe because that box of people was the safest and most survivable place to be (plus you might have found that special person to be with, or at least someone who didn't want to enslave or kill you). Mental Boxes were, therefore, a remarkable innovation as a quick way to categorize and sort sensory information and keep you safe. Those skills for putting things, animals and people quickly and accurately into categories - mental *"boxes"* - were literally a matter of life and death throughout much of human history.

What we are suggesting, however, is that they perhaps no longer serve us in the way they used to, and we need to be aware of the good, bad, and ugly boxes. From that point of awareness, we must now make conscious choices about who and what we put in boxes and understand the consequences of those choices. Awareness and choice - these are the twin forces that pierce through the assumptions and fallacies that often come with box-based thinking.

Ever heard us talking about boxes on the radio, a podcast or interview? Then you might have noticed that we're often asked a question along these lines:

So, Rúna, Nick and The Change Makers, you've got this #NoMoreBoxes movement going on, but at the same time, you're saying not all boxes are bad. You're saying, in fact, that some of our boxes are brilliant and bring us enormous amounts of joy and keep us safe. So why the #NoMoreBoxes movement? Why "**No More**"?

And you know what? That's a valid point.

It should probably have been something more like the *#NoMoreBadLimitingDivisiveUglyCruelUnkindBoxesBut-KeepTheGoodOnes*movement. But somehow it didn't feel quite as memorable. Plus - and this is important - when we started out on this journey, we had a lower awareness or sophistication about boxes (compared to our thinking now) so we might have come up with a different name for the movement if we were starting again. But we are happy to stick with #NoMoreBoxes because it opens up this broader, deeper conversation.

So, the box-based thinking was helpful and useful early in human development and, in fact, made our survival more feasible. But let's fast-forward to the present day and see what happens, shall we?

There are two features of 21st-century living which make both the creation and persistence of boxes even more likely than before. These two aspects of our present-day lives make boxes more deeply embedded in our way of thinking and how we make sense of our surroundings and the people in it.

First of all, the world has become a whole lot busier and vastly more complex than ever before. This creates an even bigger temptation to put things and people in boxes.

Without these boxes, our thinking processes could become quickly overwhelmed. (Oh, for the simpler days of picking fruit, catching wild tofu, and hiding from hairy men in unisex bearskin underpants!)

A study conducted by researchers at the University of California-San Diego estimated that between 1980 and 2008, the number of bytes of information consumed by humanity rose by an astonishing 350%. (Bohn, R., & Short, J. (2009). *How Much Information? 2009 Report on American Consumers.* San Diego: Global Information Industry Center of University of California, San Diego.)

And here's the really incredible thing: this was before the explosion in social media usage throughout the world. Today, we're literally bombarded by a torrent of ideas, opinions, and facts presented through sound, imagery, text, and more, all day and all night long. Our human minds have to filter all of this information and make sense of it.

The result? We're even more likely to categorise things and put them in boxes, grouping things and people together. Without it, our minds would simply be unable to cope with all that we were exposed to. We'd go "POP!"

On top of all this, we've got yet another set of boxes to contend with: all of the boxes created by historical circumstances. As we travelled through time, we've brought with us loads upon loads of historical and cultural boxes from past generations and people. We've got layers and layers of history mingling in with our current thought structures, limiting our ability to make clear, informed, and unbiased decisions, or to see the world accurately as it is. And this situation might get even more staggeringly complex as we program machines through the constraints of our current biases and boxes.

Consider, for example, this fascinating question that was posed to the manufacturers and programmers of Artificial Intelligence Assistants: *"Why do the majority of those devices have a female voice?"*

Their answer was telling. They replied that the female voice is deemed more helpful and supportive and in a position of service. OMG! We're adding gender biases right into the *"smart"* machines we're creating, thereby perpetuating the crude, box-like notions that men hunt, and women serve.

So, although not all boxes are inherently bad, we've got to be really careful that we're not carelessly building more boxes on top of historical boxes and biased thinking patterns creating a wall we'll never get over. We need to be alert to the very real, very alarming possibility that we're sleepwalking into yet another layer of boxes.

But how we can cultivate this alertness - this awareness - within ourselves?

Thousands of years ago, a Chinese military genius, called Sun Tzu, offered one possible answer to that question. In his legendary treatise, "The Art of War", Sun Tzu wrote: *"If you know the enemy and know yourself, you need not fear the result of a hundred battles. If you know yourself but not the enemy, for every victory gained you will also suffer a defeat. If you know neither the enemy nor yourself, you will succumb in every battle."*

To heighten your awareness of box-like thinking, and to help you win this battle against Bad and Ugly Boxes, we're going to adopt Sun Tzu's advice. You must know yourself as well as the enemy - the enemy being undesirable box-like thinking. To that end, we've identified 8 fundamental drivers that create boxes (and yes, we are making some boxes of our own with these eight categories!).

We'll discuss these key drivers in more depth in Chapter 7, but for now, have a look at this list of the 8 Main Drivers that Create Boxes. As you go through this list, be aware that nearly every box has multiple drivers, as well as the potential to have Good, Bad, and Ugly outcomes.

8 Main Drivers that Create Boxes

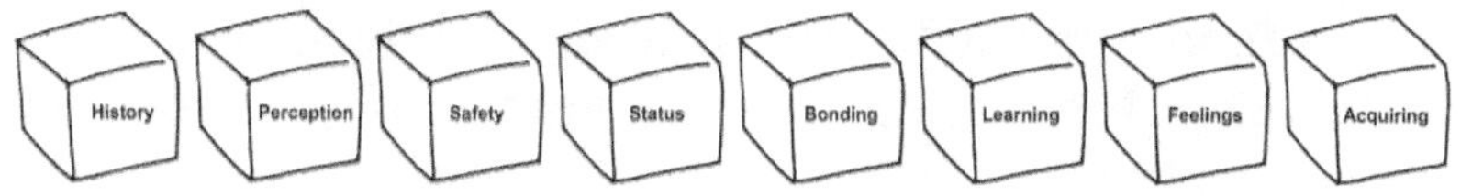

1. **Boxes Driven by History.** These boxes have formed over a very long time. Some of the reasons for their creation may have been forgotten or are now irrelevant, but their very history gives them a reason to exist. These boxes are often seen as the glue that holds things together - or, in other words, our heritage.

2. **Boxes Driven by Our Perception.** Our internal or external worldview drives the emergence of some boxes. Our beliefs, values, personality type, culture, unconscious mind, and so on, all drive us to put people and things into boxes.

3. **Boxes Driven by a Need for Safety, Security, and Defence.** These are the boxes that make us feel safer, more secure or allow us to defend what we have.

4. **Boxes Driven by a Desire for Higher Status.** These boxes elevate our status in the eyes of society or our peers. They make us look or appear better than others and give us an ability to wield influence and power.

5. **Boxes Driven by Desire to Bond or Align.** Boxes can be an incredible source of bonding and alignment with others by giving us a common cause to champion or shared interests to unite around.

6. **Boxes Driven by Learning or Understanding.** All boxes are ultimately about classification, so some boxes are driven by a desire to learn and understand through common groupings.

7. **Boxes Driven by Desire to Experience Feelings.** The drive behind these boxes is a desire for emotional experiences like fun, freedom, comfort, and excitement. For example, participating in a club or team can yield incredibly interesting experiences and associated feelings.

8. **Boxes Driven by Desire to Acquire or Obtain.** Certain boxes give people overwhelming advantages over others - lending them the power to acquire material possessions like houses, cars, and other goods, as well as immaterial forces like power and influence. These boxes often limit people who exist on the outside.

As you can see, we're driven to forge boxes for many reasons. That's why they are so invasive and infiltrate every area of life. In fact, once you start looking for boxes you can't help but see them everywhere. They come in all sorts of shapes and sizes and are sometimes Good, sometimes Bad, and sometimes downright Ugly!

For now, just observe any boxes you see and perhaps try to work out what drives their existence.

But don't judge. Just observe.

31

Your Notes:

Chapter 3

The Trouble With A Great Idea

"Energy Follows Focus - The danger of placing women in the 'Feminine Box' and men in the 'Masculine Box' is that we are saying all women are this and all men are that - when we are in fact all different and unique. That simple gender classification creates isolating and divisive boxes, and as a result, limits humans to be the change they want to see in their world."

~ Rúna Magnúsdóttir, founder & CEO The Change Makers co-creator of the #NoMoreBoxes Movement

---

Alright then, you've learned a bit more about some of the drivers behind boxes and the biological reasons why we have this urge to put people and things into these invisible boxes. Now you're ready to dive deeper into an exploration of the different types of boxes - the Good, the Bad, and the Ugly Boxes that shape our thoughts and behaviour.

It's important for you to wrap your head around these three types of boxes and really get to know them, because only when you are more aware of your boxes will you have a deeper understanding of how they influence you. You'll also be in a much better position to alter, disrupt, and even destroy - if necessary - the boxes in your life.

This awareness also grants you a kind of superpower: the ability to consciously move among the Good, Bad, and Ugly boxes that fill your mindscape.

There's something else we feel we should mention here. We're going to share stories about boxes with you and analyse these stories, too. However, we do this while wearing a non-judgmental hat. Judgment, after all, often assumes the shape of box-like thinking. We also encourage you, our dear reader, to thoroughly open yourself to pure, raw learning free of judgment, so that you may more richly untangle the meaning and implications of the many stories of boxes we'll share with you throughout the book. There is an adventure in that kind of learning.

As you've discovered by now, there are a lot of different sorts of boxes out there. Because of that, it's challenging to choose one specific box to use as an example of the Good, Bad, and Ugly sides of boxes. So, we decided to begin by looking at a box that is perhaps a very delicate one to talk about. It is nevertheless a box that we must face is causing a paradoxical mix of tranquillity, peace, and joy for many, while also producing profound darkness, intense isolation and loneliness.

Now, with that said, are you ready to dive into these boxes, and get more than just your feet wet?

We'll begin by sharing with you a very personal story from Rúna. This is a story about the 'Gender Box', and in this case, the driver behind the box was a particularly sneaky one: the perception driver (the way we see and interpret the world).

Rúna: "As a forward-thinking, active and extremely driven female entrepreneur, I've always believed I could have the best of both worlds. In other words, I've held a strong conviction that I could independently earn my own living and also have a family. The mingling of these two boxes, the box of the female entrepreneur and the box of the family, has been very empowering for me. But it wasn't always that way.

As a young woman, I placed myself in very limiting and lonely boxes. I was in a relationship where I didn't feel wanted as a woman because the man I was sharing my life with had a totally different understanding of what constitutes intimacy and desire in his life than I did. Because of this, I placed him into the "Male Box" - or, rather, I should say I put him in the *"he-is-not-a-man-with-a-normal-sexual-drive-Box"* I believed a rule that a man *should* sexually desire his partner in life. As a result of this belief, I felt ugly, unloved, undesired, isolated, and just plain lonely.

Years later, I now realise that I had put us both into a rather ugly box that caused real unhappiness. In all honesty, I now see that what really happened was this: two very different people had deep feelings for each other, but their sexual drives weren't aligned.

That's all it was.
Putting him into that destructive box - based on my belief about how a man should be like - and placing myself into the *"I'm a victim"* box or the *"I'm not an attractive woman"* box isolated both of us.

And that ended the relationship.

Now, I'm not going to lie and tell you that it was easy for me to accept all of this. It took a lot of time and reflection to understand that my thinking and my feelings had been shaped by these boxes. It took time for me to see things the way I see them now. And the first step towards this new, clearer view was understanding that the boxes in my past relationship were created by me, myself, and I. Then I dug deeper into my own thought processes and discovered just how much of these boxes were driven by my own perception, and that perception is subjective. Perception is based on the perceiver, and any given perception is not the truth for everyone.

As I said, this wasn't easy at all. Abandoning one's earlier convictions can be a very, very uncomfortable experience. However, once I left these boxes (like the box of feeling like an unattractive woman), I had the liberation and space to move forward. What I also realized later is this: the moment I let go of this limiting and lonely box, I was also liberating my ex. Knowing that gave me an even better feeling.

As you might have gathered from just this story alone, boxes can nest inside each other - not unlike a Russian Doll. Open up one box, peer inside, and you'll often find another box hiding within. In this story, there was the Gender Box, characterized by Rúna viewing her then partner as beholden to social expectations for what a man should be like. Inside that Gender Box lay the Relationship Box, in which Rúna felt unloved because of her partner's lack of affection. And deeper still lurked the *"I'm-not-an-attractive-woman"* box. The driver behind all of these boxes - responsible for causing all this drama - was simply perception.

In the next chapters, we'll share a good number of stories that reveal the dazzling diversity of boxes that exist. We encourage you to ask yourself the important questions while reading this book - questions shine a light on the boxes operating in your own mind.

What is so fascinating - and, at the same time, so disturbing - about our various boxes is the fact that they are often totally invisible. But, in this case, out of sight doesn't mean out of mind. These hard-to-see boxes determine our automatic reactions to so many different situations and thus play a large role in our wellbeing.

Let's take a moment to consider another box we're already familiar with: the Education Box. Just like most other boxes, there are Good, Bad, and Ugly sides to the Education Box. It isn't an altogether "Good Box"; in fact, it can at times be a really bad and even ugly box.

Why do we say this?

Consider this, for example: when a young child isn't so good at art (in the conventional, institutional sense of the word *"good"*), that child will be told that it's no big deal, it's just not their thing, and their potential for success in life won't be impacted.

On the other hand, though, if a child isn't (conventionally) good at math, then there's a good chance that child will be seen as slow, stupid, and not likely to be as successful in many areas of life!

These are two different skill sets, both of which are hugely valuable to the world. However, the student who has math skills at a young age is placed in the "Smart Cookie" Box that empowers them in life. Meanwhile, the student who fails their math's classes is more likely to land in the *"What-the-f@ck-are-we-going-to-do-with-this-one"* Box.

One box is liberating; the other is a hindering locked cage. And yet the great, vast world outside of institutionalized education needs both art wizards and math mavens.

If we don't wake up to the ugly side of the Education Box and change our reactions and judgements, we will continue to forge a society where so many people don't stand up for themselves, thrive, and blossom in whatever profession they choose. And because of that, we'll still have a society where, being unhappy with their lives, so many people turn to drug and alcohol abuse and even commit suicide.

Think about your own life; your history, your family, and friends. Who has suffered because they weren't valued or accepted because they were placed in the limiting Education Box? And if these stories ring a bell for you, then you may have found yourself in a similar situation - enclosed within a box. Or, perhaps and hopefully you have already stepped out of the box.

Stop for a minute or two and ponder this: You can always move your boxes around! These boxes you're reading about aren't made of concrete or steel. They are not unbreakable. Why? Because they're made out of something far more malleable: your imagination and your perception.

For instance, in Rúna's story above, she let go of her fixed perceptions - thus moving her boxes around - and this gave her space to open up to the woman inside. By doing that, she feels like she's moved from an "Ugly" Gender Box to a "Good" Gender Box.

Doing the research for this book has been such a transformative journey for us, the authors. We've come to notice how our exploration of boxes has started to help us address the unconscious behaviours and biases we live with, and that this exploration is a nonstop process. And as the *Rule of Attention* states, whatever you put your attention on grows in strength, which is another great reason why this has been a remarkable journey for us.

Working on this book helped us further develop the idea for the awareness movement, and also to design the process within the **#NoMoreBoxes Breakfast Clubs™**, creating a really safe space for people to come together in their organisation's kitchens or canteens and have deep, meaningful conversations about their boxes.

When we were further refining the process within the **#NoMoreBoxes Breakfast Club™** meetings, one of the participants, Kristin Sigrun told us: *"One of my biggest takeaways from this meeting is that I now feel like I have accessed a brand new language - the language of these universal boxes. As an HR manager working with all sorts of people from all walks of life, the 'Box Language' gives me a beautiful way to understand where others are coming from and communicate openly and respectfully with other people."*

If you find the **#NoMoreBoxes Breakfast Club™** an interesting concept, keep reading - we'll be sharing a whole lot more about the movement with you later in this book.

And if you'd like to dig into more stories of boxes, amble over to Chapter 8. But before heading that way, put a bookmark of some sort on this page so you can come back and continue learning more about the drivers behind boxes, and how we can move forward as a society.

In the next chapter, we'll look at a 3-step process to help us move away from boxes that no longer serve and towards and into boxes that nurture and empower.

CHAPTER 4

HARRY HOUDINI AND THE GREAT ESCAPE

"The Secret to Happiness is Freedom…
And the Secret to Freedom is Courage

~ *Thucydides*

As we started to write this chapter we thought again about the "No More" component of the **#NoMoreBoxes** movement, and that we should have gone with a hashtag that expressed more precisely what we mean; The *#NoMoreBadLimitingDivisiveUglyCruelUnkindBoxesBut-KeepTheRest* movement. To indicate that we're taking a stand against the boxes that don't serve us or are cruel or divisive. So, I want you to hold in your mind, that despite our crazy hashtag, not all boxes are bad and there are some boxes that we can absolutely love being in and wouldn't ever want to leave.

You might love being in the *"I am a Mum or Dad Box"* or be really proud to be in the *"Nurse Box"* or even walk around with a smile on your face because you're in the *"I Love Small Cute Dogs Box"*. There are boxes we adore being in and we're not suggesting that they are wrong or that you should leave them. Don't worry, be happy!

We're merely proposing that we become more aware of the boxes around us, and then assess if they are Good, Bad or Ugly for us, others or society as a whole, and then decide if we want to change that.

This book is about Human Liberation, Peace and Happiness for all of us, and the role that boxes play in that. With that said, let's start exploring a process to increase your awareness about boxes. From there we'll move onto how you can move from the boxes that no longer serve you into the boxes that nurture you and move you forward.

Keeping it simple!

**"For I am a bear of very little brain,
and long words bother me."**

~ **A.A. Milne,** The World of Winnie-the-Pooh

Once you start to open up your thinking to the world of boxes and their impact on all of us, it can at times move from a beautifully simple concept into a maze of questions, and at times, a bit of a muddle.

Is this box, Good, Bad or Ugly for me, and has it always been like that? How did I get into the box in the first place? Did I put myself in the box? Surely not! Or was it society, my parents or the box monster?

As you start to explore this whole subject of boxes, we can move from the simple idea that boxes exist, into something far more complex, and at times confusing.

The first thing to say is, *"that's normal"*. Once you've let the cat out of the box, so to speak, it can open you up to 101 questions and thoughts.

To help with this, we've developed a simple **3 Step Framework** to enable you to become more aware of the boxes around you and assess if they are Good, Bad or Ugly. From that place, you can decide if you want to escape that box or enjoy being there.

In the next part of this Chapter, we'll outline **The 3 Step Framework for Human Liberation, Peace and Happiness** for you and then in **Chapter 5** break it down further and walk you through it with a series of exercises. For now, let's just look at the framework, with its rather grand title!

The 3 Step Framework for Human Liberation, Peace and Happiness

Step 1: Awareness - Be Curious and Spot the Box

Guess what? You're already here! The first step is simply becoming more aware. In a way, the whole #NoMoreBoxes movement is about this starting place. Becoming more aware that boxes exist and that they can be brilliant or the cause of many of the world's challenges around division, inequality and isolation. In this first step of the process, all you are really doing is opening up your thinking and observing.

In **Chapter 5** we'll take you through some exercises to help with increasing your awareness, but for now, just be curious and observe. Perhaps you can cheekily eavesdrop on conversations and see which boxes you start to see. Remember, it is important not to judge when you start to see people in their boxes or give yourself a hard time about your own boxes. Just stay open and be curious.

Come join our Facebook Group and meet other people at this stage of open curiosity. You'll find us at www.facebook.com/groups/nomoreboxes

Step 2: Understanding - Get to Know the Box

Sometimes it can take a while to get to know someone or for something to become clear. Other times you can know and understand someone in an instant. It's the same with boxes. Step 2 is all about getting to know and understand the boxes around you, which could be an instant recognition and knowing, or a longer process of discovery and adventure.

Once you've seen a box, your next thoughts and questions might be...

How did I get here?
Why am I in this box?
What are the drivers that lead me here?
Who put me there?
Was it me, or someone else?

And after that, it's time to explore questions like these

Is it a Good, Bad or Ugly Box? (or a mixture of those)
How does it serve me?
How does it serve others?

What are the benefits and advantages of this box?
Does this box bring me happiness or joy?
If so, how?
How does this box harm or limit me or others?
What are the disadvantages, limitations or issues around being in this box?

What would my life be like without this box?

In **Step 2** of the process, we take you through a series of questions and exercises to help you work all of that out, or at least enough to help you make choices from an informed position. We'll also make sure you have some fun and not feel overwhelmed at any stage.

When we've completed **Step 2**, you're ready to move on to **Step 3.** This is where you can decide if you love or like your box and want to enjoy it some more, or if it's not serving you as well as it could. We'll also discuss how to escape the box or adapt it.

Step 3: Action - Love, Leave or Live with Your Box

"The greatest escape I ever made
was when I left Appleton, Wisconsin."

~ **Harry Houdini,** magician, escapologist, stunt performer

Personally, we quite like to the look of Appleton in Wisconsin. It sits at the top of Lake Winnebago and by all accounts is a rather nice place to live. That's the point of **Step 3.** It's all about you and what is right for you.

In **Step 3,** you'll have worked out if particular boxes serve you or not. If you find yourself in a box that you don't want to be in, this next step takes you through a process which helps you Escape or Adapt your box. Sometimes this can be a breeze and a simple choice, but that box can also prove as stubborn as a mule at an ice cream stall, completely refusing to be broken.

If you're not a mind-bending Houdini, escaping a certain way of thinking or being can be quite tricky. Boxes may trap us, but they can also feel familiar and have a sneaky habit of making us feel safe and reassured. Change can be difficult.

To help you with any challenges you may face in **Step 3** we're going to use something called *Conscious Questions,* which is an innovative and popular tool developed and used by Nick over the last 35 years in his clinical practice. *Conscious Questions* also form the cornerstone of Nick's upcoming book, ***Feeling Good About Yourself.***

So, let's get Nick to explain exactly what *Conscious Questions* are, and how they can be used to open up your thinking and overcome any resistance or fear around change or escaping your box:

One of the difficulties we have, when we try to remove, dismantle or change the contents of our boxes, is that once our boxes have formed, they nestle deep in our Unconscious Mind working away like a secret machine - classifying everything and everyone into their respective boxes. And it's well recognised that trying to change anything in your Unconscious Mind or your unconscious driven behaviour is notoriously hard to do, which is where *Conscious Questions* come in.

Conscious Questions have the ability to tap directly into your Unconscious Mind, and while there, alter your stored memories, beliefs and perceptions - including any box you have nested away. Conscious Questions do all of that by utilising one of the Unconscious Mind's functions - to answer questions. The Unconscious Mind is constantly working away answering any questions it's asked, and here's the important bit, ONLY the question it's asked, and nothing else. It doesn't try to flip it around or change the question, it just answers the question.

So, if for example, you asked, *"Why are men so cruel?"* then your Unconscious Mind would answer that question and tell you why men are cruel. The Unconscious Mind isn't looking for a balanced view - that's unless you ask it for a balanced view, and then you'd get one.

If for example, you asked, *"Why are some men kind, and why are some men cruel?"* your Unconscious Mind would tell you why that's true.

So, you can consciously construct a question that will give you a more balanced or helpful view of anything you choose to look at, including boxes.

And that's what Conscious Questions are.

A *Conscious Question* is any question that you ask on purpose, in a mindful or conscious way, that is designed to get a helpful answer.

A helpful answer would be one that inspires you, empowers you, calms you, relaxes you, excites you or creates a more balanced view of yourself or others. It could also give you a solution to a problem that you're struggling with or a simple way to move forward.

***Conscious Questions* and Personal Empowerment:** Another powerful use of *Conscious Questions* is in the area of personal empowerment, and the ability to rise above any box that tries to hold you back.

To look at this let's go back to the fact that your Unconscious Mind has to answer any question you ask, and that you also have a brilliant, wonderful and powerful Imagination that also has to answer any question you ask - and again only that question, nothing else.

So, if for example, you asked, *"Why am I so stupid?"* then your Unconscious Mind would answer that question and tell you why you're stupid, and your Imagination would join in and start to make up all sorts of rubbish in its attempt to answer that question too.

But what if you were to ask, *"Why am I powerful?"*

What would happen then?

Your Unconscious Mind and Imagination would tell you exactly why you're powerful, and as a result, you'd feel more powerful and act that way!

Now let's look at an example of a set of boxes that I was put into - the You're Bad At Languages Box and the Dyslexic Box and see how *Conscious Questions* can help shift my thinking around those boxes.

As a child, I was told repeatedly that I wasn't good at languages because I was dyslicrix and struggled to remember lists of words. As a result of those boxes, I never really tried in any language class and now when I go abroad, I often rely on them speaking English, which isn't good.

So, I could ask, *"Why am I bad at languages?"* and get the answer to that question. Or I could ask, *"What would be a fun way to get even better at speaking Italian?"* and get my Unconscious Mind to first recognise that I have a certain level of Italian - so I'm not all bad - and my Imagination to come up with all sorts of ideas to get even better!

We're going to use *Conscious Questions* throughout this book as a way to help you identify boxes and as a simple, powerful and painless way to escape them - if that's what you want to do.

Conscious Questions in Action

Using *Conscious Questions* in Step 3: Action - Love, Leave or Live with Your Box

Below is an example of the *Conscious Questions* we used to help a woman named Sandra when she reached **Step 3** of the Framework.

Sandra had uncovered - in the previous two steps of the framework - that she had the police in a box that said: "Police are untrustworthy and bend the law to suit themselves".

This notion came to her from watching television programs in the 1990's, seeing video phone footage of the police beating people up, and because a previous boyfriend of hers had been a policeman and had repeatedly cheated on her. This view that the police were untrustworthy was starting to become problematic at work for Sandra because she had to deal with the police on a regular basis in her role as a Social Worker, and one of her co-workers was married to a policewoman.

So, we suggested that Sandra ask the following three *Conscious Questions.*

Question 1:
"Why are there some corrupt police in the world?"

Question 2:
"Why are there some very honest police in the world?"

Question 3:
"Why are we lucky to have the police force?"

By asking these three questions, stacked one after the other, we forced her Unconscious Mind and Imagination to find the answers to those questions and as a result, give her a new and more balanced view of the police.

If you'd like to learn more about *Conscious Questions*, and how they can help you dismantle your boxes, build your self-esteem and navigate through life then head over to www.ConsciousQuestions.com/boxes

***Conscious Questions* are life changing!**

In the next chapter, we'll take you through some more exercises and the **3 Step Framework** in more depth. Then, in **Chapter 6,** we're going to explore some more of the challenges as well as the benefits of escaping or adapting to the boxes that you find yourself in.

Actions: For now, just be open and curious about boxes and what they might mean for you and the world around you.

Perhaps ask this simple *Conscious Question.*

"What boxes are around me?"

See what shows up.

Your Notes:

CHAPTER 5

WE LOVE IT WHEN
A GREAT PLAN COMES TOGETHER

"Who do I want to belong to and identify with? Those who put others in boxes - or those who don't? Although I'd like to be someone who never puts others in a box, I still do it - which is why it can be uncomfortable to be a leader. A courageous leader relentlessly pursues self-awareness - even if it means admitting that you're imperfect and still make plenty of mistakes."

~ Margareta Kull, creator of The Courageous Leader

In one of our **#NoMoreBoxes Breakfast Clubs™** which explored the Gender Box, there was a gentleman in his late 50s named Bill. Bill had a powerful 'Aha!' moment when he discovered how his unconscious biases influenced his actions.

During the Breakfast Club meeting, Bill talked about his belief that society will take a step in the right direction when far more women make up the next generation of global leaders. He underscored the importance of seeing more women take leadership positions in both the business and political arena.

On a rational level, Bill thought that this was the way forward for the world. But when he dug into his core beliefs about who a "woman" is, and looked openly and honestly into his 'Woman Box', he realised something startling: deep down, his view of women really wasn't about leadership at all. On the contrary, Bill's idea of who a "woman" took on the form of someone who takes care of children, cooks, cleans and is beautiful. And when he examined his core beliefs of who a "man" is, he saw someone who is competent, strong, and a leader.

It was amazing and insightful to watch Bill's newfound awareness surge to the front of his mind, shedding a light on how he was subconsciously placing women into a box that didn't give the women around space to become the leaders he said the world needed (even though he considered himself a feminist!).

What's more, he began to realise that if he saw a woman act as a strong and powerful leader, he viewed her as less feminine - less of who she "should" be.

Uncovering these deep-seated beliefs was quite the experience for Bill, who felt disturbed and confused as he sat quietly and observed his new understanding of the world. *"There is a lot to think about,"* he said.

Truth be told, when we're running a **#NoMoreBoxes Breakfast Club™**, it's difficult at times to witness people have these (sometimes) disturbing realisations about their own thought patterns. But there's a silver lining. We know that relief and salvation are just around the corner for these brave individuals who have boldly ventured into the vast, unexplored frontiers of their own minds. The feeling we get when we see this is similar to what a schoolkid feels on a Friday afternoon, knowing that the weekend and freedom is coming.

As for other participants who watch someone come to grips with their newfound boxes? Perhaps it's like watching an exciting thriller, wondering, *"How is the protagonist going to get out of this hair-raising situation?"*

But how do we know that relief and salvation are just around the corner? How can we be sure that the hero will win the day just in the nick of time? Because of **The 3 Step Framework for Human Liberation, Peace and Happiness**, which we discussed in the last chapter!

So, let's explore that **3 Step Framework** further, using a man called Bill as an example. You'll see how this approach helped Bill delve into his hidden beliefs and how he managed to hop, skip, and jump out of his confusing Gender Box like a lamb on a spring day.

Here's what went down - and what his escape plan looked like!

Step 1: Awareness - Be Curious and Spot the Box

Bill was curious enough to explore the idea of boxes, and could thus spot his own Gender Box, which he was subconsciously using to categorise men and women into distinct roles. And particularly that women are kind, caregivers, homely, better at listening and more empathetic.

Step 2: Understanding - Get to Know the Box

"How did I get here? Why am I in this box? Who put me here?"

These are the kind of questions Bill asked himself to better understand his box. He immediately saw that one of the main drivers of his box, labelling women as beautiful, caregiving housekeepers - was his upbringing. In other words, his box was driven by perception; an internal worldview that was cemented in his mind at a very young age.

Bill was raised in a family of six in the 60s and 70s when traditional beliefs about gender roles prevailed in many homes. So even though his mum worked outside of the home, his views were nevertheless shaped by mainstream society's ways of thinking.

Bill didn't stop here, though, and pressed forward - trekking deeper into Box World. He wanted to know if his box was Good, Bad, or Ugly, or some kind of mixture of all three. Overall, he felt that his Gender Box had both good and bad sides to it.

When asked, *"How does this box serve you?"*, Bill struggled to see how having women in a caregiver role served him, or anyone for that matter.

He was then asked, *"How does this box NOT serve you?"* Bill sat for a while, quietly thinking. After a long pause, he wiped the sweat from his forehead and said, *"Because it doesn't match what I know to be true. I'm not at all aligned with it."* Then he added, *"It actually disturbs me big time because each time I meet a woman that doesn't fit into that box I feel disappointed in them and that they had failed in some way".* By his own admission, he said he felt that those women were hard, unfeeling and less womanly, whatever that means!

His discomfort was obvious, but not surprising, as it can be uncomfortable to discover something about yourself that you were so unaware of.

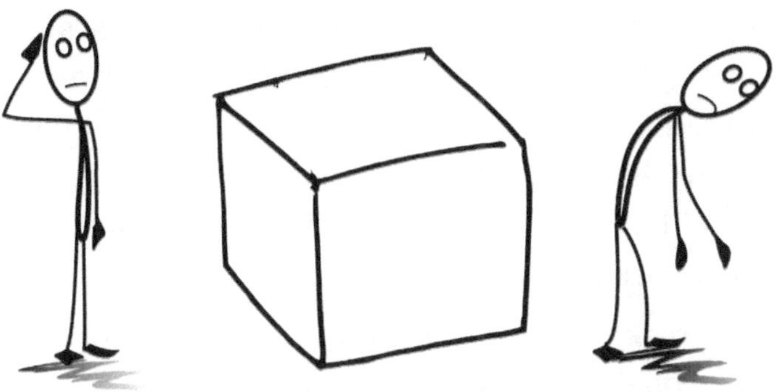

Since the purpose of this method is to help raise your awareness of boxes, with compassion and kindness, it's vitally important that we discuss the third and final step of the process. This is where the real turnaround and transformation happens.

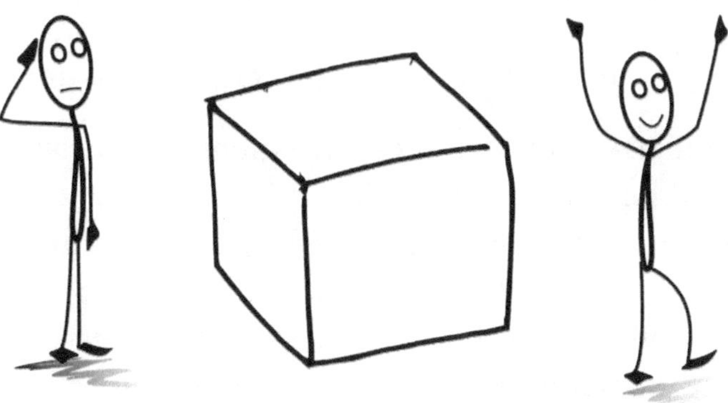

Step 3: Action - Love, Leave or Live with Your Box

To kickoff Step 3, you've got to work out for yourself the answer to this question: *"Do I want to continue living in this box, because it serves me, or I love living in it? Or do I need to escape this box or adapt to it in some way?"*

In Bill's case, he really wanted to escape his Gender Box, so he would no longer be tied down by traditional, faulty beliefs. We decided that getting Bill to ask a series of *Conscious Questions* would be the best way to transform Bill's thinking in a kind, loving way. This would help him understand himself better (a good thing for everyone to learn) and help him let go of his fixed beliefs and all their negative consequences.

We, therefore, encouraged Bill to ask himself these three *Conscious Questions* - one after the other - and see what, if anything, shifted in his mind:

Question 1: *"Why are some women caring, and some less caring?"*

Question 2: *"Why do lots of women have strengths that lie outside that area?"*

Question 3: *"Why is it good that people are different?"*

When Bill asked himself these questions, his unconscious mind and imagination got to work searching for answers. And those answers did come to Bill, opening his mind to a new view of the world. He started to form a more balanced view that the qualities of being caring and listening did not have anything to do with gender.

Note: if someone's core beliefs are especially entrenched and practically "locked in place," we encourage them to ask themselves their *Conscious Questions* each day for a week.

Remember, change takes time and repetition is powerful!

By using Conscious Questions, you can gently escape your box and move into a more fulfilling, empowering, and nurturing box. A box that's a lot more fun to live in! In fact, that's what happened to Bill. In his case, it clearly served him to put his old beliefs to rest and escape his box.

But what if your box has no escape? What if, for example, someone in your family has an incurable condition - a potentially limiting box for which there is no easy way out? In cases like that, we suggest adapting to that box instead of attempting The Great Escape.

Let us give you an example of how one can adapt to a box. Consider Kathy, a lovely grandma with Alzheimer's disease. For her and her family, there was no escaping the fact that she had Alzheimer's, but they could modify their thinking and response to the disease. Let's explore that a bit more by moving through the **3 Step Method** again.

Step 1: Awareness - Be Curious and Spot the Box

When Kathy's family opened up about the Alzheimer's Box, they talked about their first reactions to the diagnosis and how they wanted to keep this news within the family. It would be too humiliating for their grandmother to be exposed to the world as someone who was losing her mind. Fundamentally, this decision came out of their belief that people with Alzheimer's needed to be protected. So, they figured the more they could hide Kathy's Alzheimer's from everyone, the better it would be for her.

Step 2: Understanding - Get to Know the Box

To more completely understand this box, Kathy's family had to answer challenging questions like, *"How did we get inside this box? Why are we in this box? And who put us here?"*

As the family discussed this, it soon became obvious that TV programs, and everything they'd read about Alzheimer's, told them that the disease was tough, hard on everyone, and embarrassing for the person with it. Then they got really honest, admitting that they were ashamed of potential odd behaviour that could be heading their way, and of the confusion that Kathy was beginning to show.

The family then tried to determine if this box was Good, Bad, or Ugly.

So, they were asked, *"How does this box serve you?"*

Kathy's daughter offered this response: *"This is a really bewildering time for all of us. So, knowing that we're going to keep Mum's diagnosis a secret, and downplay her behaviour to protect her, gives us a level of certainty because we've got a plan. Plus, it feels safer since we'll be doing what everyone else does."*

Next, the family was asked, *"How does this box NOT serve you?"*

They all sat there in silence for a while, and then Kathy's eldest grandson said, *"It's not how Nan would have approached it. It's like her life is all over before it is."*

Joan, a life coach and Kathy's daughter-in-law, replied that keeping grandma's condition a secret would be much worse for everybody, especially for Kathy herself, since people would talk about her behind her back. Other people, unaware of the diagnosis, would also be unsure how to behave around their grandma.

Step 3: Action - Love, Leave or Live with Your Box

In this case, the family needed to adapt. They couldn't escape the Alzheimer's Box, but they could change what they put in that box and how they lived within it.

It was at this step that Joan suggested that the diagnosis should not be kept a secret. Instead, she said, they should openly talk about their grandma's journey, and even laugh with her at her comments and soon-to-come changes in behaviour. Joan noted that their grandma was indeed a patient with Alzheimer's, but she was still grandma, - who always loved making fun of herself. *"Why should we take that away from her?"* she added. *"Loving and supporting grandma as she is - no matter what - will bring our family closer together. And other people will be more at ease when they interact with her."*

At that point, a giggle went around the room. *"Grandma, do you remember when you said sausages and cream instead of strawberries and cream?"* asked Joan. Kathy smiled.

In Chapter 8, you'll read some more of our favourite stories of people in real life and throughout history - people just like you - who have taken these 3 steps to heart so they could become the change they wanted to see in their world.

CHAPTER 6

THE ANCIENT CHINESE ARE IN THE BUILDING!

"I know what the fear of not fitting in can do to you, your well-being, and your performance. Because when you're ridiculed for who you are, you sometimes choose to fly under the radar - and not make any waves or stir things up. And yet, interestingly enough, the moment I was at peace with who I am, nobody seemed to mind. In fact, many people were inspired. I started to look at people unconditionally - and, in turn, people saw me in the same light. That's when I got my taste of what life can be like when you're free - when you're living outside the walls of the boxes."

~ Gido Schimanski, Paradigm Shifter for High-Achievers

"You can't teach an old dog new tricks" is a pithy saying you might hear when someone's talking about changing habits and behaviours. But we'd like to challenge that old platitude, and even create a new adage: "If you're going to teach an old dog a new trick, first give the dog space to understand why this new trick is beneficial."

'Giving Space' and 'The Benefit'

"Giving Space and *The Benefit* are two vital topics we're going to explore in this chapter. In short, before moving from one box to another, it's helpful to give yourself the space and freedom to figure out the personal benefits of making that move. When you do that, you'll be in a much more determined and in a better headspace for letting go of old boxes that do not serve you or keeping the box and reconfiguring it, so it moves from a Bad or Ugly box to a Good version of the box.

Why take the plunge and risk leaving the safety of your Box?

To a great extent, society constantly urges us to lock other people into various boxes with an endless stream of judgment. When you look around it might seem as though just about everybody is obsessed with lumping people into different boxes. Try paying close attention to what politicians are really saying, for example - so much is about putting people in boxes.

The status quo of box-based thinking seems set in stone - or can certainly feel that way - so why should you rock the boat? Why should you make the effort of moving yourself and others into a box? After all, you can be safe and sound by staying in your own little box and avoid the risk of being ridiculed by society. You won't have to run through the gauntlet of sharp comments and remarks that some people might make if you shake society's boxes, or feel isolated because others decide to place you in a box because they think you're different. In short, why should you stand out from the crowd - and put yourself out there by attempting to break free of the boxes that rule your life? You might be asking yourself *"Is it really worth it?"*. We get it. It can take a whole lot of courage to act on what you believe. Things might seem much easier if you just go with the flow, letting somebody else take the risk of disrupting the established order.

Although it can be comfortable to let things stay the way they are and not ruffle any feathers, we urge you to ask yourself this: *"How are my automatic reactions (the ones that put people in these limited, isolating boxes) serving me today? Are they giving me a feeling of fulfilment, inner joy, and peace? How are my boxes NOT serving me today?"*

In our view, there are many good reasons for raising awareness of one's boxes, biases, and automatic reactions. For example, this heightened sense of awareness can open doors to new opportunities in your life, give you greater freedom, a more inclusive worldview, and people will probably love and value you more as you let go of your Bad and Ugly boxes.

You see, we believe that when you raise your own self-awareness, you are building a world where you are more accepted for who you are - because you will be more open to accepting people as they are.

As we noted earlier, it can absolutely seem challenging to move from one box to another. It's easier to do that, though, when you first give yourself the space to discover the personal benefit of going from a Bad or Ugly version of the Box to a Good version of Box.

How can you create space to grow yourself?

Marcia Martin, philanthropist, thought leader, and co-creator of the Network of Transformational Leaders says: *"Space and things in space: the two things that make all the difference. If you don't have space where new things can exist, nothing will change."*

Consider this: if your wardrobe is filled with clothes, you'll need to take something out to make room for the new trousers you bought, right? The same holds true for your headspace. If your head is full of fixed, rigid thoughts that no longer serve you, you might find yourself in such a small box that you can barely breathe! Put differently, if you aren't all that open to learning and exploring, chances are good that you don't have any space to soak in new knowledge and experiences. So, the willingness to learn new things about yourself, or understand yourself and others better, is how you can give yourself the space you need for meaningful personal growth.

Opening yourself up to this self-exploration can take on various forms. But whatever form that takes the key is always unabashed openness.

Here's a case in point. One of Rúna's clients, Daniel, a financial executive at an insurance company, came to her with a request: he wanted her to help him make up his mind about whether or not he should leave his job.

Daniel told Rúna: *"I've been working hard to get to this point in my life, and although I am well-paid at this job and have all the material benefits I could want, something is missing. I'm wondering if it's time for me to move on."*

To tackle this conundrum of his, Rúna suggested that they take a look at his personal brand by going through the 360° Reach Personal Brand Assessment (an assessment where 30-40 people in his network gave their feedback on how they see him). Throughout this assessment, he gave himself the space to discover how people saw and experienced him, as well as how he saw and experienced himself.

The results were quite interesting.

For one thing, his family and close friends saw him as a funny, relaxed guy. But those qualities didn't shine through when he was with his professional colleagues. Instead, they saw Daniel as a serious guy and a strategic doer.

After this assessment, Rúna had a deep discussion with Daniel about these differences in how people perceived him. This conversation was his space to explore. That's when he realised why he wasn't feeling completely fulfilled and satisfied at work. The assessment allowed him to see his own blind spots - and helped Daniel understand how he had put himself into a limiting box (with the drivers of history, safety, perspective, and bonding). Simply put, he believed that if he was to be respected as a professional, he could not be funny.

He needed this space to grasp that he was holding himself back from truly being his authentic self.

When Daniel realised that this was his own doing, he decided it was time to get rid of that limiting box. So, he and Rúna came up with a simple strategy to eliminate that box from his life; a step-by-step process where he recognised the benefits of showing his humour at work.

So, did things change for him? In short, his work life was transformed. As Daniel moved from a limiting box to the Good Box of showing his funny side at work, he started to feel fulfilled, loved, and valued as his colleagues saw him in a different light.

It wasn't the company or the people in the company that were getting in his way of satisfaction at work. It was his own doing, putting himself in a limiting box that he himself had created and put himself into.

"Whether you think you can, or you think you can't —you're right."

~ **Henry Ford,** Founder of the Ford Motor Company

Henry Ford made a good point about our belief system. Historical figures, people long gone but whose wisdom has stood the test of time, can often provide us with insights that ultimately give us a more meaningful and happier life in the here and now. So, in this chapter, we'll explore the benefits and challenges of escaping any box that doesn't serve you by taking you to ancient China, 2,500 years ago.

This section of the book is taken from Nick's life work. Nick has spent his complete adult life working with and exploring ancient Chinese medicine and philosophy to help individuals, businesses and society as a whole to be kinder to themselves and others and to navigate, survive and thrive in the modern world.

Throughout most of his 35 years in private practice, he had at least a 6-month waiting list of people who wanted to work with him, which at one point reached a ridiculous 2-year wait. We hope you enjoy and value his thinking, wisdom and experience as you navigate your way around the world of boxes.

In China, about 2,500 a years ago, great thinkers like *Confucius* offered fresh perspective on the art of living. It was during this remarkable time, which became known as the *Hundred Schools of Thought* that various Chinese philosophers proposed that everyone is born with a specific energy makeup, a unique blueprint, composed of Five Energies: Water, Wood, Fire, Earth, and Metal. The specific balance of these five energies determines how you see the world or respond to any situation you find yourself in. It is because we all have different energy types that two children or adults can have exactly the same experience, but nevertheless interpret it in radically different ways. (This viewpoint is the same system used today as part of traditional Chinese medicine and related healing arts.)

So, what does this system of Five Energies have to do with boxes - and your great escape from a box you don't want to be in?

Well, to a large degree, your Energy type determines how you can escape a box - and it is often the reason you fell into a particular box in the first place. Let's dig into that in more depth.

To begin, we'll introduce something called the *"Big Question."* A Big Question is a question you're driven to ask yourself over and over again. Each Energy type has their own Big Question. The answer to your Big Question speaks to something that really, truly matters to you, and it explains why you see the world in a particular way. Your Big Question is like your window on the world.

Below you will find the Big Question for each of the Five Energies. After you look through these questions, we'll discuss how they impact your ability to be a modern-day Harry Houdini, allowing you to escape your undesirable boxes:

The Big Question for:

Water Energy is *"Am I - or are we - safe?"*

Wood Energy is *"Am I - or are we - free?"*

Fire Energy is *"Am I loved and appreciated for who I am?"*

Earth Energy *"Do I understand and am I understood?"*

Metal Energy is *"What is missing or incomplete?"*

Now that you've gone through these Big Questions for each Energy Type, it's time for some stories.

As someone whose primary energy is Water, Janet kept asking her Big Question: *"Am I safe? Are we safe?"* She was always focused on all-around safety, both for herself and others. When Janet started to examine her Career Box, she realised that she had never really challenged the box her family had put her in, because she was scared.

At heart, she was a lover of food and art - and would have loved to have had a tea shop with cakes, treats, and perhaps a little gallery on the side. But what did she do instead? She was a doctor.

Of course, there's nothing wrong with being a doctor - after all, for some people, it's a dream profession. But it just wasn't for Janet. So how come she ended up as a doctor?

From day one, her family had put her in the Doctor Box, believing that, to be safe in this world, you have to have a good education and a secure, respected job. So, growing up, Janet worked towards being a doctor. It was an easy sell too because her family told her that she'd be as a doctor she would be safe. This tapped right into the Big Question of her Water Energy. Even when she recognised that she was in this rigid box, the thought of being anywhere else terrified her, so she decided to continue doing a job she doesn't like. The tea shop on the other hand? It's sitting somewhere in her mind as a retirement dream.

Now consider the case of Sai. Sai is an entrepreneur, as was his father and grandfather before him. It's what men do in his family, and he loves living in the Entrepreneur Box especially since it suits his dominant Wood Energy with its Big Question of: *"Am - or are we - free?"*

As a father, Sai is also eager to see his daughter Myra forge an independent career and not tie herself down with marriage. This is typical of Wood types like Sai, as they want freedom for everyone, and this perspective makes it easier for him to hop, skip, and jump out of the Gender Box. But it's not all smooth sailing in the Sai household.

Here's the thing: although Sai wants his daughter Myra to be an entrepreneur - what better life for a young, free, and modern woman, after all - Myra actually wants to be a teacher. Her dominant Energy is Earth, and with her desire to understand and be understood, the thought of entrepreneurship, with all its unknowns and uncertainties, fills her with horror. But teaching in a school? Oh, what fun!

In this situation, Sai's Wood Energy drives him to seek freedom - so he loves entrepreneurship and easily breaks free from the Gender Box - but it also pulls him into thinking that the Entrepreneur Box is ideal for Myra.

For Fire types, the Big Question is: *"Am I loved?"* Going against the norm of their family or society can therefore be a real challenge for any Fire type who must escape a box. Take Frank, for example.

Frank loathes the Ugly Locker Room Box with a vengeance, with its talk of women as sex objects. In fact, it makes him feel sick to the stomach - as it would any man who's got a couple of brain cells.

The problem? He's a Fire type who works in commercial property, where it's all about who you know. Plus, if he's honest, he really cares what people think about him and he wants to be liked. So how can he step up and take a stand against what's wrong with the Ugly Locker Room Box so common in his type of business, and risk being disliked and possibly compromise his livelihood?

When the Change Makers were speaking at Impact Leadership Global Summit 2018 (held at the United Nations Headquarters), there was a strong and wise man on the Conversation with Men panel, Brent Hamachek (CEO of Segueway Solutions, Inc.). When this subject of taking a stand came up, he said, very simply, that sometimes you just have to do what's right. Even if it costs you and you're going to be unpopular.

One of the reasons why we're are sharing with you these stories about people and their Energies is this: sometimes your Energy type can make it extra hard for you to break out of a particular box. Sometimes, to take a stand against a certain box, you've got to put on a pair of big blue girls' underpants and feel and be uncomfortable.

Finally, Metal Energy, with a story about Mandy and how she sought to escape her box that said, "Dyslectrics, Dislextics, Dystectics... ah, that's right...Dyslexics are stupid."

Like many Metal Energy types, Mandy was a perfectionist, relentlessly asking herself the Big Question: *"What is missing or incomplete?"* The manager of a big department store, Mandy struggled with her biased perceptions of graduates or new staff members who had any level of dyslexia and made any kind of spelling mistake. She immediately wrote such people off as stupid. And although Mandy tried to see the value of neurodiversity in the workplace, she just couldn't get over this perception she had about spelling and intelligence.

These stories illustrate that when we know our Energy type, it's easier to understand where our biases, boxes, and perceptions come from and why we might struggle to release them.

If you'd like to find out your Energy type for free, just visit this web page: www.fiveinstitute.com/nmb

There, you'll find a link to take **The Vitality Test** developed by Nick over the course of 35 years of work in this field. It's easy to take the test and we promise it'll open you up to a whole new way of thinking about the world and understanding your boxes (whether they're Good, Bad, or Ugly)!

CHAPTER 7

LITTLE ERIC AND A GRAIN OF SAND

---

*"If we are to succeed at breaking down any boxes,
we must first strive to understand others
before needing to be understood ourselves."*

~ Susanne Frandsen, Creator of The Magnetic Leadership
Program

"Are you alright, Eric?"

"No, not really, Martha. I've got an awful lot of sand in my underpants - and I think some of it is trapped beneath the foreskin of 'little Eric.'"

"Oh dear, poor you. Why don't you do what Barry did?"

"What's that, Martha?"

"Well, he got Keith the Knife to whip off all that loose skin, and problem solved - no more sore, sandy, little Eric."

"That's brilliant, Martha! Barry sure is a bright chap! And I've got an idea Martha: if we're blessed with a son, let's make sure that Keith the Knife sorts that out for him too, and let's not wait till our son is all grown up. Let's get it sorted when he's a baby - perhaps just after he's born."

"That's brilliant, Eric - I knew I'd married you for a reason!"

Now, we the authors aren't 100% sure that we've completely and accurately nailed the exact conversation that led to the origin of the Males Should Be Circumcised Box. But, regardless, that box clearly exists.

So, when Rúna watched *Cut: Slicing Through The Myths of Circumcision* - a documentary film by Eliyahu Ungar-Sargon that examines the subject of male circumcision from a religious, scientific and ethical perspective - she was brought to her knees with distress. Sobbing, she asked herself: *"How come this ritual that started in the year 500 B.C.E, most likely for hygienic reasons, is still practised today despite the fact that the myth that circumcision gives rise to good health is constantly busted by doctors and scientists? Circumcision takes away a great deal of a man's sensitivity and his ability to be a fully sensuous human being. How can parents take away their sons' right to choose what he wants to do with his penis? What if it was their child's ear - would that be acceptable to cut off?"*

The answer to Runa's question is, of course, *"No*: it wouldn't be ethical to do that to your child's ear". But, although that seems obvious to us, and many other people, others continue circumcising their sons without giving it a second thought. That's how powerful boxes and the drivers behind them are. In short, certain boxes - those driven by history, for example - encourage questionable things to happen and beliefs to perpetuate way beyond their sell-by date. So, in this chapter, we're going to further explore the powerful drivers that lead to the Good, the Bad, and the Ugly Boxes, including the drivers that caused the demise of *'little'* Eric.

8 Main Drivers that Create Boxes

1. Boxes Driven by History. These boxes have formed over long periods of time. Some of the reasons for their creation in the first place may have been forgotten, or may now be irrelevant, but their very history gives them a reason to exist. These boxes are often seen as the glue that holds things together or, in other words, our heritage.

Practically anywhere you go, you will encounter boxes driven by history. They are extremely pervasive because they've had a lot of time to build up, accumulate, and cement themselves within a society's psyche.

They are also extremely insidious. For one, people will often be reluctant to let go of these boxes because they create the illusion of personal and interpersonal stability and provide a surface-level sense of who we are and where we have come from. Such boxes are therefore frequently perceived as normal and thus go unquestioned and unchallenged. They are, instead, vigorously defended - sometimes to the death - for it is incredibly tempting to use these boxes to define our identity and guide our actions and lives. For example, the story of *'little'* Eric and the Males Should Be Circumcised Box illustrates a typical box driven by history: it both defines certain cultures and is often unquestioned and unchallenged.

From the standpoint of the Five Energies, it is quite common for someone with Wood Energy to either valiantly defend or vehemently attack these historically-driven boxes. If you will recall, the Big Question for Wood Energy types is, *"Am I - or are we - free?"*

Because of that desire for freedom, Wood types can lose their sense of perspective when they believe their freedom - their right to choose - is about to be taken away. And if they think that an injustice is being committed, or someone's liberty needs to be defended, then they will be up in arms to fight the good fight.

Thus, you'll often see Wood types on either side of the argument about a historical box, often becoming more and more entrenched in their thinking and less and less inclined to enter into open dialogue or debate. So if you've got lots of Wood Energy, look out for that!

2. Boxes Driven by Our Perception. Our internal or external worldview drives the emergence of some boxes. Our beliefs, values, personality type, culture, unconscious mind, and so on, all drive us to put people and things into boxes.

Once you've accepted a given perspective as valid, it can be very, very hard to clearly see things in another light. Thus, boxes driven by one's initial perception of things, such as the Wealth Box *("people that are poor are X" or "people that are rich are Y"),* can become a fixed and normalised part of our mental makeup.

For example, think of all the films that put all poor people in one box (as the struggling heroes, perhaps) and rich people in another (maybe portrayed as people who need to be brought down a peg or taught a lesson). Both of these perceptions can be dangerous, unhelpful boxes that trap and limit people, even if they are sometimes used for entertainment purposes.

So, what's the secret to breaking free of the boxes driven by our perception of the world? The key here is to increase your awareness of your own biases and understand where they come from.

Consider the story of Janet. Janet was a wonderful lady living in the west of England who'd had a difficult childhood with extreme bullying at school. Her biggest stress, however, wasn't the bullying - although that was horrific - but the fact that the teachers didn't listen to her when she told them what was happening. So, as she grew up into, she placed every teacher in a box that said: *"Teachers aren't caring or understanding."*

Although based on quite a sweeping generalisation, this box Janet created didn't cause her any great problems. Until that is, she met and married Frank who - after 10 years of marriage - said he wanted to be a teacher!

When Janet took the Vitality Test, she found out that she was a dominant Earth Energy type. Her Big Question was: *"Do I understand? Am I understood?"* That explained why it was easier for her to forgive and forget the bullying, while she had a harder time letting go of a past where many teachers didn't listen or understand her.

This realisation, however, did allow Janet to move on from the box she had put all teachers in and, after 3 years of training, Frank became a teacher (and Janet is now considering joining him!).

Our Energy type (along with other factors) drive us to perceive that some people should be in a certain box and others shouldn't.

3. Boxes Driven by a Need for Safety, Security, and Defence. These are the boxes that make us feel safer, more secure or allow us to defend what we have.

The need for safety and security - as well as the desire to defend what you have - is recognised as a fundamental influence in human societies. This same need drives the creation and continued existence of many boxes. In brief, we create and uphold boxes that make us feel safe and secure and that allow us to defend what we think is ours. One such box, for instance, is the Nationality Box.

The Nationality Box makes people feel safe and secure by uniting them under a shared national heritage. However, things can get ugly quite quickly within the Nationality Box, as it is often used to manipulate society's thinking and to advance a particular political agenda or ideology. How does this manipulation happen?

The Nationality Box groups certain people based on a simplistic set of traits and qualities; those who do not have these traits and qualities are considered *"outside"* the box, and thus a threat. So, people outside the Nationality Box are frequently stereotyped and dehumanized by those within, which, historically, have been the first steps to some of the worst atrocities ever committed.

Water types are the ones most susceptible to be driven by a need for safety, security, and defence. Water types with their Big Question: *"Am I or are we safe?"* will have a natural focus here.

4. Boxes Driven by a Desire for Higher Status. These boxes elevate our status in the eyes of society or our peers. They make us look or appear better than others and give us an ability to wield influence and power.

"I refuse to join any club that would have me as a member."

~ Groucho Marx

Belonging to certain boxes - an elite club, for example - can immediately elevate your status in your own mind and in the eyes of others. And as the desire for status is quite fundamental to human nature - and is often linked with safety (another powerful driver) - it probably does not come as much of a surprise that we have a world of boxes driven by status. Status Boxes can include a profession or membership in a special club and can bring great joy, but also become a tool of exclusion that unfairly keeps other people out.

Nick's father, Tony, loved cricket (along with gardening and his work as a physician). In the 1960s, Tony had the privilege of becoming a member of the Marylebone Cricket Club (MCC), a centuries-old cricket club with an 18-year waiting list for membership!

On specific days of the year, he'd put on his orange and yellow MCC tie and head off to watch cricket (and escape his five children). There was a respect for the MCC tie, and people who saw him as he sat on the bus knew that he was a member of an elite and passionate cricket club. He was in the MCC Box and he loved it. Until, that is, the mid-1970s.

The problem he had with the MCC? It couldn't move with the times: the membership voted against the idea of giving women full access to the club wanting, instead, for the MCC to remain as a club just for men.

At that point, Tony handed back his treasured membership to the MCC in protest - and put away his tie. It wasn't until 1998 - more than two decades later - that the MCC finally allowed women to apply and join the 18-year waiting list (at which point Tony also re-applied and brought out his MCC tie in excited anticipation of rejoining the club and his now more inclusive box).

The lesson here? It's good to enjoy your boxes, but many Status Boxes are built around excluding others, a hallmark feature to look out for any time you catch yourself in a Status Box.

5. Boxes Driven by Desire to Bond or Align. Boxes can be an incredible source of bonding and alignment with others by giving us a common cause to champion, or shared interests.

A former greengrocer from the U.K., Christopher Crawcour, has amassed one of the largest fruit sticker collections in the world. His rarest stickers include 1960s-era labels from the giant banana distributor Chiquita. Although his wife doesn't share his love of fruit stickers, there are plenty of people around the world who do.

This is but one example of the many ways people can bond over a common passion or cause. Personally speaking, neither of the authors quite get fruit sticker collecting, but then again, many people don't get Rúna's and Nick's shared passion for collecting half-used tins of paint.

In short, whether you're a collector of fruit sticks or half-used tins of paint or a member of Greenpeace or some other group devoted to a cause, in many cases you're probably driven by the powerful need to bond and align with others.

Yet boxes driven by this need are not always so faultless. Sometimes, such boxes can validate behaviour that is unacceptable and abhorrent, as in the case of the 40-year-old paedophile ring in the sleepy British town of Telford, where more than one thousand kids were found to have been abused since the 1980s.

6. Boxes Driven by Learning or Understanding. All boxes are ultimately about classification, so some boxes are driven by a desire to learn and understand through common groupings.

There comes a point when we're talking about the 8 Main Drivers with people when we suddenly see smiles and nods appear around the room, as if things have, all of a sudden, become a whole lot clearer. Because these 8 drivers have been categorised into their own, distinct boxes, it's easier for people to make sense of a complex and (at times) confusing set of patterns. And that's one of the reasons why boxes can be incredibly useful: they can help us learn and grasp the complex and confusing. They help us navigate and comprehend a world that constantly bombards our senses with an incredible amount of information.

But like many other boxes, boxes that are driven by a desire to learn have Good, Bad, and Ugly versions. These boxes are also often favoured by certain energy types.

For example, Earth types - with their desire to understand and be understood - will frequently have the urge to classify things into neat little boxes, thereby making sense of them. So, word to the wise: be mindful of this urge if you happen to be an Earth type.

There's something else to be aware of when it comes to boxes driven by the desire to learn: sometimes, when we place something into one specific box, it can be challenging to move it to another box when the need arises. Let's explain this a bit more.

Take the Gender Box, for instance, and the habit of labelling certain qualities as either feminine or masculine. We've looked at this before, but it's worth revisiting. When you say that a focus on collaboration is a feminine style of leadership, then you've subtly excluded the thought that men, too, can be collaborative leaders. On the flip side, when one classifies control and command as a masculine leadership style, then the idea that a woman can exercise such a leadership approach has been suppressed, even if only a little.

"Women are collaborative, caring, co-creators"

Well what happens if you are a woman and you are not, or you are a man and you are collaborative, caring and a co-creator?

Be aware of the advantages and disadvantages of putting something in a box when trying to understand and learn. By approaching boxes driven by this desire with awareness, you'll actually broaden and deepen your ability to comprehend the world around you.

7. Boxes Driven by Desire to Experience Feelings. The drive behind these boxes is a desire for emotional experiences like fun, freedom, comfort, and excitement. For example, participating in a club or team can yield incredibly interesting experiences and associated feelings.

If you're ever in Nottingham and need to know how much it costs to have your car's upholstery professionally cleaned after two very smelly teenagers have sat in it after camping at a three-day music festival, Nick can tell you that it's £53.20. And then the car will still have a rather smelly aroma!

Which, in a roundabout way, brings us to the next driver: the desire to share common feelings and experiences.

A desire for positive feelings is a powerful driver and can lead us into many boxes of commonality. We join clubs, hang out with like-minded people and sit in a mud-soaked field for three days surrounded by leaky toilets. In short, we all like to experience fun, freedom, comfort, and excitement and such feelings are often enhanced and intensified when experienced with others within a group or box. Fire-types in particular have a penchant for sharing common experiences and enjoying the intensity of emotions.

So, does the drive to experience feelings create any Bad or Ugly boxes?

Indeed it does! Like many other drivers, the desire to share common experiences can become a Bad or Ugly box when it excludes others, isolates people, or validates harmful, hurtful and despicable behaviour.

In 2014, it was revealed that as many as 1,400 children were sexually abused by a paedophile ring in the north of England. In 2016 eight of those men were found guilty of waging what prosecutors called an "utterly abhorrent" campaign of sexual violence and intimidation against girls. A box that validated, supported and allowed some of the most despicable behaviour imaginable.

8. Boxes Driven by Desire to Acquire or Obtain. Certain boxes give people overwhelming advantages over others, giving them the power to acquire material possessions like houses, cars, and other goods, as well as immaterial forces like power and influence. These boxes often limit people who exist on the outside.

They say the good die young, but actually, it's the poor. The drive to acquire or obtain is a compelling one and often the reason people aspire to be in a certain box. Your box could mean that you live in a wealthy part of the western or eastern world, or that you're a member of a box that gives you access to resources and wealth beyond other people's means.

Some people, for example, send their children to elite private schools, not because the quality of education is particularly better, but because it puts their children in a box that gives them access to people and opportunities that will help them acquire more.

We - the authors - have no judgment on that, but the observation and recognition stands that some boxes make you richer. By doing so, such boxes - if they are exclusionary in nature - can make other people poorer. The reverse also holds true: if you're in a box that makes you wealthier, it's not a given that that box is Bad or Ugly. It could be a generous, kind, and world-changing box, something that we applaud, as the central theme of this book is to explore those boxes that don't serve us and celebrate the ones that do.

In the next chapter, we'll uncover the boxes that have come close to destroying the world, as well as the boxes that have led to greater liberation.

CHAPTER 8

PERSONAL POWER COMES TO TOWN

---

*"As I was growing up in East Germany
- when the Berlin Wall was still standing strong
- I came to the realisation that most of the walls in our lives
are actually created by our own minds.
So to grow as individuals
and become the best version of ourselves,
we must deliberately dismantle those walls."*

~ Monique Blokzyl, Business Launch Portal CEO

Throughout this book, we've mentioned that we, the authors are a part of the Change Makers, an international group of thought-leaders and business experts who have come together with one, unequivocal mission: to empower humans to be the change they want to see in their world.

That's the purpose of our existence as Change Makers, the purpose of the global #NoMoreBoxes awareness movement, and the reason behind the launch of the **#NoMoreBoxes Breakfast Clubs™** around the world.

It's also why we wrote this book.

"The only thing necessary for the triumph of evil is for good men to do nothing."

~ Edmund Burke

We feel that it's never been more important for humanity to wake up and take responsibility for our individual and collective actions on a day-to-day basis, thereby being and living and breathing the change we want to see in our lives and across the world.

And if perchance you are thinking to yourself, *"Well, I'm pretty powerless. I can't do much because of X, Y, or Z"*, then think again, because in this chapter you'll read surprising, inspiring stories about change-makers worldwide. People like you. People like us. People who have let go of their limiting boxes and harnessed their personal power.

But before we get to that, let's take a good, hard look at the really ugly situation we'll find ourselves in on this planet if we, as a society, as a species, and as intelligent, thinking creatures, don't step up our game.

Consider this: what will happen if we don't do anything about our unconscious biases and behaviours that place people - including ourselves - into very limiting, isolating boxes?

Well, the answer is not sweet at all. In fact, it tastes quite rancid. You see, if we continue on with this business-as-usual attitude, never raising our awareness about our boxes, you can be sure that human civilisation won't be finding peace and happiness anytime soon.

Staying inside the walls of the status quo will affect your unborn children or grandchildren - and their children, too. Not just you or me or your friends, but everyone else currently alive on this wet-and-round chunk of rock-in-space we call home.

By keeping ourselves and those around us shut inside constraining boxes, our families and communities will be left with more unhappiness, more suicides, more depression and alcohol and drug abuse as people feel disconnected from who they truly are.

As more and more people feel isolated and limited no matter where they turn, we will see fewer and fewer people prosper and thrive - whether materially or mentally. Fewer businesses will flourish, too, as their human resources remain stuck in limiting boxes, with their greatest talents repressed. And with less productive human resources in the workplace, businesses will see flatlining profits, and in turn drop the employees' salaries and make it even harder for businesses to hire qualified people.

The result? Communities, cities, and countries will have a larger number of unemployed people. More unemployment means more people will be forced to rely on their government for social care (if they are even lucky enough to live somewhere that has social care). There will be more poverty, and there will be more starvation.

How ugly is that?

That's not all. We will see many other really ugly stories played out to in more intense and more insane ways. We are already witnessing such things as young children being torn away from their parents who are only seeking a safer, better life in another country for the people they love. Children separated from their mothers all because of a single act by the President of the United States, Donald Trump. Who may be grappling with the challenges of his own Status Box.

We will continue to see fierce friction from those in the Masculine Box who are fighting hard against the Feminist Box frightened of losing their status-driven box in a society that prizes status and power over anything else. In reality - outside the illusory world of boxes - members of both of these boxes are really only striving to be heard and valued. The endless dialogue about *'US vs. THEM'* is slowing down the process of gender equality (not to mention equality for all). It's actually creating a deeper gap between the genders and people on the whole.

None of the staunch champions of either Gender Box is listening to what the other side is saying because their respective views often come down to sweeping generalizations about what each gender should be, have, or do. They just keep shouting at each other, unloading their own frustration and anger because they don't feel like anyone from the other side is really listening to them. (Hey, let's face it: there's a lot of truth to that because members of the other box are just waiting for their turn to talk and vent.)

Then there is the subtle and not so subtle embedded racism that exists every day on our streets, in our work, governments, prisons, schools, in our policies and nesting deep within the boxes within our unconscious minds.

And all of this won't just affect human beings. It will impact everything on this planet because violence and warfare (and these two very frequently result from limited, ugly boxes) cause immense damage to the planet's biosphere and environment.

So, here's an interesting question — or perhaps it's more of a riddle — how much longer are we going to keep up this madness?

If you're like us, the authors, you're sick and tired of this situation. We sincerely hope you are taking to heart the importance of stepping up your own game. That could mean, for example, creating your own action plan by looking at the things you want to see changed in the world, starting, as the King of Pop said, with the man in the mirror.

At this point in the book, we're pretty sure you understand the seriousness of the situation. You understand how dangerous and ugly the future will be if we don't do something about our own, often unconscious, behaviours and ways of thinking.

'Be the Change You Want to See In Your World'

~ **Gandhi**

But it's not all bleak.

Not at all, actually. There's a bright-and-sunny side here: there are thousands upon thousands - make that millions

- of people who have, for one reason or another, decided to be the change they want to see in their world.

People, for instance, who have decided that they want to be free from boxes - even if they don't refer to them as such. Or people who want to liberate others from boxes and create a world that is more equal and fairer.

People like Dr. Martin Luther King, Jr., who wasn't born with a silver spoon in his mouth, but who nevertheless confronted a divisive, unfair social system with extraordinary vigour and courage. Dr. King created a movement that liberated humans with his world-famous *"I Have a Dream"* speech. His dream was a world without all the limiting boxes of race-based oppression.

Or consider the story of Malala Yousafzai: This young girl who captured the attention of the whole world after narrowly escaping with her life when the Taliban tried to kill her because she was unafraid to stand her ground and demand that girls be given equal access to education.

Then there's Oprah Winfrey. Oprah was born in the midst of poverty, yet she's used her story to inspire, coach, and mentor millions of people of worldwide so that they can escape any box that holds them back.

And finally, there is the amazing and inspiring Hawk Newsome who is the president of Black Lives Matter, Greater New York. We met Hawk at the United Nations event where the #NoMoreBoxes was born, and he is probably one of the most amazing men either of us has ever met. After telling the stunned and shocked audience of the breathtaking injustice, horrors and crimes against his black community by white people and the white system, he proceeded to passionately call for a coming together to talk and breakdown the barriers that divide us. Hawk can clearly see and dream of a world without ugly and divisive boxes of race and colour.

None of these people, you will note, were born with a stamp on their forehead saying, *"A Super Powerful Changemaker."*

However, just like you, they were born with a special gift unique to them.

All of their stories reveal that they - at some point in their lives - decided that there should be no more ugly, limiting, and isolating boxes, and they would become the change they wanted to see in their world.

**"When the whole world is silent,
even one voice becomes powerful."**

~ Malala Yousafzai

Now, you might be thinking to yourself, *"Yeah, but these people are the exception to the rule. These are the world-famous people, and I'm not world-famous."*

Be aware though, that this is a limiting perspective in itself. And, as Malala so brilliantly reminds us all in that above quote: it all starts with one voice - and our world needs your voice, too.

That being said, let's have a look at a few stories of boxes from so-called *"normal"* people (oh what a boxy sound the word *"normal"* has).

For example, there's the story of Brynjar Karl, an autistic Icelandic boy who is changing his world by painting his Autism Box with bold, beautiful, powerful colours. Brynjar Karl is doing that by sharing his love for two things: making things out of Lego cubes - and the story of the Titanic. His simple act of sharing these two passions of his by building the [something about the size of] Titanic out of Legos has given hundreds of thousands of families across the world deeper understanding and appreciation of the beauty of the Autism Box.

If you are not familiar with Brynjar Karl's truly astonishing story, just do a Google search for his name and you will see how this young autistic boy has been changing the world by empowering people, raising awareness of the Autism-Box. Brynjar Karl is sharing his story of, how he used his 'Autistic X-factor', as he calls it, to make his huge dream, to build a replica of the Titanic ship with Lego cubes, come true.

Brynjar Karl kept going, in pursuit of his dream, no matter what. And once the ship was built, he and his mother, Bjarney Ludviksdottir (one of The Change Makers) with great help from his grandfather Ludvik Ogmundsson, have been sharing his story, thereby helping other families with children with autism to discover just how good the Autism Box can be, empowering other families to embrace the unique gifts of their loved ones with autism.

Another amazing individual, and a change-maker, is Preethi Herman. Preethi is from India, and she is the Global Executive Director for Change.org. Preethi grew up burdened with a horrific fear. From the time she was nine years old, the Indian movies she watched told her that if a girl was sexually assaulted, she'd have to kill herself to save her family's honour. As she grew older, she found herself increasingly trapped inside boxes that were driven by history and culture.

In an interview in *Times* (May 2nd, 2018), Preethi recalled a memory of arguing with her neighbour who told her that women had to be subservient to men since womanhood is a punishment for a transgression in a past life. She was told that her most important duty in this world was to be an obedient wife.

In Preethi's mind, that was simply not an option. So, instead of becoming the obedient wife, she finished her studies and travelled alone, lived alone, and made her own way in the world. None of that gave her the approval of her native society, but now she was free of those ugly boxes.

Today, as a valuable executive for the Change.org Foundation, Preethi has helped the organisation grow from less than 200,000 members to over 10 million. She now leads a passionate team that seeks to ensure that people throughout the globe have a voice which can take on the issues affecting their communities.

Preethi's team members are in Asia and Latin America, fostering communities of change-makers, turning the media's spotlight towards critical issues, and working with politicians so they understand the power and significance of grassroots activism.

Another great example comes from the bestseller *Blink: The Power of Thinking Without Thinking* by Malcolm Gladwell. In the book, Gladwell tells a story that shows beautifully how you can change an Ugly Box into a Good Box (in this case, the drivers are perception and the need for safety, security, and defence).

This astounding story occurred in the world of classical music. Elite orchestras would hold auditions to determine which musicians would get to join. Traditionally, the audition committee would sit and watch as one musician after another came in and played. Most of those that got hired after the auditions were men.

Few people gave this a second thought. It simply meant that men were generally better musicians, right?

Then someone had the idea of holding blind auditions, placing a screen between the judges and the musician. That way, the audition committee would have no idea who was actually playing. At first there was no change in the gender balance - still more men were chosen over women. Then the researchers realised that the judges could hear the sound of the musician's shoes as they walked across the stage, identifying who was a man and who was a woman. So, they asked every potential candidate to remove their shoes before they walked across the stage. Almost immediately after this change, there was a dramatic uptick in the number of women who were hired.

This story elegantly illustrates how complex our biased boxes can be.

Finding the Fuel

As authors and members of The Change Makers, we've shared much of our motivation for writing this book and why we are so passionate about the #NoMoreBoxes movement.

We mentioned, for example, how we're both incensed by injustice, how we loathe division and cruelty, and how we hate the thought that future generations will be trapped in boxes. We discussed, too, that we long for a world where understanding prevails, where everyone has the freedom to be themselves, unconstrained by all these made up boundaries and classifications that don't serve any of us. And, of course, we want this planet, the only planet we as humans can call home, to survive and thrive, not blighted by pollution, warfare and violence, and possibly mass extinction.

All of this fuels us to get up in the morning, to do scary things and to step into a place where we feel, at times, very vulnerable and very exposed.

There's another *"special fuel"* we use that drives us to challenge the boxes that are all around us and are embedded into so much of society. That fuel is kindness. We know from firsthand experience that it's far kinder to each and every one of us if we choose to step out of our boxes and allow others to do the same. It's kinder to the planet, too. Imagine, just how powerfully and effectively as a combined force we could tackle climate change if each of us weren't limited by our boxes or the boxes that divide us.

As such, we began this riveting journey by approaching the question of boxes through the lens of kindness. (This should be no surprise since Nick is an International Kindness Ambassador by profession and Rúna is by nature a kind and considerate person.)

So, with that in mind, we want you to continually ask yourself these three questions as you start exploring the boxes in your life:

1. *"Is living in a box being kind to me?"*
2. *"Is putting someone in a box being kind to them?"*
3. *"Is letting Bad and Ugly Boxes exist unchallenged kind to the planet?"*

Although you might not be world famous, an international changemaker, a civil rights leader, or a boy that found his X-factor, you certainly have the capacity to be *as kind as kind can be*! And that, in our opinion, is probably the most important and wonderful fuel for change. The strongest force for breaking down the Bad and Ugly Boxes around you and embracing the Good Boxes. Choosing Kindness!

Chapter 9

Boxes And The Business Of People

"My first female boss - who was a good mentor most of the time - told me I was 'high-strung' and that I needed to cap it. I later learned that was code for: 'Don't speak up as men do. Be a nice, polite little girl who waits to be spoken to.' That's a box that many women are in - and have been in for decades and decades. So, the sooner women break out of this box, the sooner they - and the companies they work at - will experience greater success."

~ Leslie Grossman, Feminine Leadership Expert

CEO Susanne: *"Hey Harry, now that Paul is retiring, we'll need new car insurance salespeople in our sales department."*

Sales Manager Harry: *"Yes, Susanne - I'm on it! In fact, I was just about to contact our recruitment partner and ask them to look for a new hire. Truth be told, it'll be difficult to replace Paul - such a great guy and a star salesman. Gosh, we're definitely going to miss him around here."*

CEO Susanne: *"Paul will be greatly missed. Make sure you keep in mind all of the wonderful qualities he brought to the team so that we replace him with someone who can easily fill his role. Oh, and one more thing: our board has made it very clear to me that we need more gender balance in our team. The mission is to make our entire workforce more diverse - and that includes the sales department. So look very closely at all applications we receive from women."*

Susanne paused for a moment, then wondered aloud: *"Really don't understand why we don't receive more applications from women. Plenty of qualified women who can sell car insurance - wouldn't you think?"*

Sales Manager Harry: *"Yeah, I really don't understand why women aren't applying, either. We even went as far as to take down the 'Girl-of-the-Month' calendar in our coffee room - and still no applications from women. By the way, I've already written down the job description, so we can get a new hire as soon as possible. How does this sound?"*

He opens a document on his computer, then eagerly reads the job description he has written to Susanne: *"We are looking for a positive, service-minded mechanic who knows how to connect with the other guys in the team. He is solution-driven, a great team player, probably loves cricket. He consistently follows up with his leads and always sells the car insurance package that's just right for the customer."*

One could hear Susanne coughing a couple of times and then see her staring at Harry with astonishment.

CEO Susanne: *"Is this description similar to what we've always used to search for salespeople for the car insurance sales team? Do we really need a mechanic for the job? The new hire will only sell car insurance, not repair cars. You know, I think I'm starting to understand why women aren't applying for this job."*

Sales Manager Harry: *"Uhhhh. Yeah, yeah, that's true - we don't really need a mechanic for this job. We've kinda put that in the job description because that's what we did back in the 80s when we hired Paul for the position - and he had that on his CV."*

Are you thinking to yourself, *"Nah, that can't be a true story?"*

Well, actually, it is!

What's more, this story only scratches the surface of the gender bias that exists in the workplace. In fact, hard as it may be to believe, the above story presents a very typical scenario of workplace gender bias, which is often, but not always, sustained by the drivers of History and Need for Safety.

If this story came as a bit of a shock to you, imagine just how much of a jolt it was for CEO Susanne - and her entire executive team - as they discovered the very limiting box they had placed their car insurance sales team in. But this awareness prompted the company's upper echelons to closely examine their hiring process and revisit every single job description put out by the company. Now, armed with a completely different approach to hiring, the company is getting much more diverse - and better - hiring results.

#MeToo - the Ugly side of the Gender Box in Workplace

When the #MeToo movement exploded in 2017 and demonstrated the widespread prevalence of sexual assault and harassment, especially in the workplace, the world started to wake up to the magnitude of the problem and exactly what had been going on behind closed doors and in plain sight!

The #MeToo revelations are a perfect example of the consequence of the Gender Box when it turns ugly and disgusting. Women were categorized as sexual objects and certain men felt they had the right to harass, assault and abuse them based on some perverted view or desire, which the authors struggle to comprehend.

There was, and still is, an additional side to the Gender Box: how we perceive genders based on this categorization of women and men. Women often feel they are trapped in a box that doesn't give them the freedom to share their brilliance with the world. Women often also feel that they need to accept sexual harassment in order to be accepted in the 'work-box', thus feeling miserable, afraid of being wrongly judged or even sacked if they did or said anything.

Men are often lost and absurdly confused by this box too. Some men believe this objectification of women and sexual harassment is acceptable because of the history of *'this-is-how-a-real-men-behave-box'* while other men are afraid of being left out of the group if they raise their voice against the behaviour that exists.

And where have the #MeToo revelations led us as a society and in the workplace?

As a result of the #MeToo revelations there is now an increased awareness and recognition of the problem at hand. We are even seeing a number of arrests and possible the prosecution of some high-profile figures. To the surprise of quite a few men, what they might think of as manly banter is actually sexual harassment. Some men even complaining that that they are now afraid to interact or be alone with women in the workplace!

The #MeToo revolution demonstrates how awareness is the absolute key to building an organisational culture that is sustainable, inclusive and magnetic.

To create a company culture that is irresistibly attractive both to your clients and your employees, regardless of what gender they feel they belong to, organizations have to create a culture where people feel they belong, a workplace where they know they are valued for who they are, regardless of their gender. A culture where both genders feel safe, equal and empowered.

This is why it's vitally important for all leaders to become more aware of the boxes that lead to disrespect, isolation and arguments because those are the boxes that cause division.

More often than not, boxes divide us - often artificially - instead of uniting us. They make it more likely that we will defend our position and fight for what we have decided is true, irrespective of whether it is. This can cause those, that don't fit into those boxes, isolation and fear.

It took a lot of bravery to open up the ugly #MeToo box. Is the work done? Can we all just sit back and relax?

No. On the contrary.

The #MeToo stories have shaken the world and created an exceptional space to look at the real reason behind them - boxes. Now is the ideal opportunity for conscious leaders to stand up and be brave and use this opportunity to open a non-judgemental conversation about the hidden gender boxes in their organisation.

Only when you and your team are aware of your own unconscious behaviours, you can take the first steps to change them. We have to be aware of the boxes that exist and the division, confusion, limitations and vast financial losses they cause.

So if you're a business owner, manager, or leader of some kind, look deeply at our unconscious behaviours in the workplace. Ask yourself: *"Do I use a particular box to select people for my team even if that box is not serving the bigger picture and attaining the outcome my organisation wants? Is it possible that I am on autopilot, automatically going along with whatever boxes exist within the organisation, instead of confronting them head-on?"*

You could also ask yourself questions like: *"Are there Gender Boxes so deeply embedded in the organisation that they not only negatively impact the bottom line but also trap my staff in roles that don't suit them (even increasing staff turnover rates)? And are these Gender Boxes potentially opening up division and misunderstanding in the workforce or perhaps acting as a breeding ground for sexual harassment?"*

There's a fairly good chance that some of these issues and their corresponding boxes will exist in your business, because the boxes that surround us are so invasive and normalised, hiding in plain sight.

The **#NoMoreBoxes Breakfast Club™** is our solution to this problem. You may well have your own in-house solutions or trusted facilitators for this type of conversation. Regardless of how you choose to tackle this issue, the important part is that you are aware that boxes exist within your organisation. With that heightened awareness, you'll be well on your way to a more profitable, stable, fulfilling, and inclusive organisation.

Now let's return for a moment to the story about Harry and his job description for the salesperson role. It illustrates that holding onto old, box-based habits can not only be detrimental to an organisation, but also a type of behaviour that's often invisible - a blind spot. Yet, while this behaviour is frequently invisible, it can nevertheless be quite destructive for a business because it prevents the organisation from finding the best people for each role.

Is Your Organisation Wasting Its Human Resources?

As we've alluded to before, we (the authors) fully understand that there will always be boxes everywhere. In fact - and we've also mentioned this - boxes can be important, and they can be beautiful, too.

However, it may be wise to keep your professional mind constantly open, constantly re-evaluating your organisation's systems and structures. Indeed, the Organisational Structure Box can easily move from a Good Box to an Ugly Box - just consider all the inflexible structures that have been created inside businesses in the form of rigid, formulaic job descriptions. Unfortunately, such Job Boxes - like many other things in life - can trip you up if you aren't paying close attention.

In short, job roles that were supposed to give clarity to the business leader, team, and the new employee are - because of rigid job descriptions - often tapping into only a fraction of the employee's potential and capacity.

By keeping your employees in limiting boxes, your organisation is creating not only limited, stunted results but it's also fostering something that's dreadfully expensive: a waste of human resources.

Thus, if you are business owner or leader, ask yourself questions like these:

How much of your employees' passion, skills, knowledge, and experience is your organisation using on a daily basis?

Do you know what drives your employees to succeed? What motivates them to action on a fundamental level?

Remember that The Vitality Test is an ideal way for anyone to understand themselves and others in a deep and profound way and is freely available to any business or individual who the wants to take it - www.fiveinstitute.com/nmb

And, of course, don't forget to ask yourself this key question: is it possible that you - and your organisation - are trapped in the We've Always Done It This Way Box (which was the case in the story above about the car insurance sales role)?

The great news is that now you've got a deeper knowledge about boxes. You also have a method that is easy to use and will help you discover your organisation's blind spots enabling you to create a powerful team that isn't boxed in by old, worn-out systems and structures.

The Race Box at work.

The world we all live and work in is changing so rapidly, with technology moving at a breathtaking speed. The rise of Artificial Intelligence and other breakthroughs create opportunities and at the same time threaten so many of our jobs.

The result is that many businesses and their workforce are stressed beyond words. Now, perhaps like never before, an agile, inclusive and **box free** workforce is a vital requirement for the success and survival of each and every business across the world.

CHAPTER 10

PLANTING THE SEEDS OF HUMAN LIBERATION, PEACE AND HAPPINESS

"The only box I'll be happy to enter one day is my coffin. But until then? No boxes for me, thank you."

~ Bjarney Ludviksdottir, CEO Eyjafilm

So here, at last, we've arrived at the final chapter of this story - the story of the Good Boxes, the Bad Boxes, and the Ugly ones. As we end this book, we'd like to open up a new beginning by exploring the ground we've covered so far and where you might go next.

**"Now this is not the end.
It is not even the beginning of the end.
But it is, perhaps, the end of the beginning."**

— Winston Churchill, British Statesman

First, we introduced you to the concept of mental boxes and discussed how boxes can help us in many ways: keeping us safe, elevating our status, strengthening our bonds with others, and so on. But as you've seen by now, not all boxes are beneficial or good. On the contrary, in fact many boxes are anything but positive. Such Bad and

Ugly Boxes can trap and limit you and others and force division among people. Some of humanity's ugliest boxes are responsible for horrors and atrocities around the world - both now and in the past.

Next, you discovered how you get into a particular box in the first-place and how your *Energy Type* can give you a particular way of perceiving and interpreting the world around you. By understanding what your *Energy Type* is via **The Vitality Test**, you can begin to unlock the doors of the boxes that trap, block or hold you back. You also learned how asking *Conscious Questions* which reach your unconscious mind can be a powerful tool to liberate you from boxes that do not serve you.

On various pages throughout this book, you got to meet several people who have done extraordinary things with the boxes in their lives. For example, you saw how a young boy apparently trapped by the Autism Box flipped the script and used his autism as his X-factor, turning him into a worldwide sensation and, more importantly, empowered him with the knowledge of just how special and valuable he is.

You also met people who have come together to explore and discuss their boxes and perceptions in the **#No-MoreBoxes Breakfast Clubs™**, and how this movement, springing up around the world, is starting to put some serious cracks in the walls of the Bad and Ugly Boxes.

If you'd like to stay up-to-date with the happenings of the **#NoMoreBoxes Breakfast Clubs™**, just go to this page: www.nomoreboxesmovement.com/nomoreboxes-events/

Finally, throughout this book, you encountered stories of the many, many boxes that can be found out there in the world: stories of boxes at home and school, in the workplace, and in business, and how these boxes impact society and civilisation at large.

So, it's been quite the journey, hasn't it? (With hopefully the odd chuckle here and there to inject some endorphins into your system, despite tackling some heavy topics.)

That's the ground we've covered in this book, but there's just one thing missing. We still haven't heard your story!

We know you have your own stories, be they startling, sad or scintillating. What's more, we know you have stories of boxes and how they've trapped you, held you back, but also ones that have given you great joy and friendships.

So that's where we'd like to go next.

In short, we invite you to share your personal stories of boxes, so that we may learn from you and get your insights about dealing with boxes. Because when we all learn from each other, we're taking small, but crucial, steps towards eliminating much of the pain, suffering, and isolation in the world (which largely exist today because, somewhere down the line, humanity started putting people and underpants into boxes).

The intent of this book was to give you a sweeping

introduction to the concept of box-based thinking. Thus, an in-depth exploration of specific boxes was beyond the scope of the book. However, our next project is a series of short books which will look - in much closer detail - at particular boxes that, in many ways, dominate the world.

The first book in this series will examine the Gender Box. Why did we choose to start with that box? It's for a fairly logical set of reasons: the vast majority of people are familiar with the notion of gender - whether they identify with a specific gender or not - so, in our own way, we can all relate to this box.

As we've touched on in this book you're reading now, the Gender Box has Good, Bad, and very, very Ugly sides to it. Thus, it's a box that's very much worth exploring so that society can start moving more decisively towards equality and liberation.

In fact, we'd even go so far as to say that if humanity doesn't boldly venture into a deeper, more meaningful, and action-oriented exploration of the Gender Box, we probably won't advance and flourish as a species, let alone protect and heal the planet.

And now, as a grand finale to this book, we ask you to do this one thing for yourself and future generations.

Start to explore the Gender Box for yourself.

If you'll remember, in Chapters 4 and 5 we discussed a three step method that lets you grow your awareness of the boxes around you, gives you the tools to assess if these boxes are Good, Bad, or Ugly, and empowers you to choose if you want to escape a particular box. So, we encourage you to examine the Gender Box with that method and see what insights you uncover.

Here's a reminder of the three steps and some guidelines.

Step 1: Awareness - Be Curious and Spot the Box

In this first step of the process, all you're doing is opening up your thinking and observing. Think about the boxes that you put different genders into, be open and curious.

Remember, you can join our Facebook Group at any time where you'll meet other people at this stage of open curiosity. You'll find us at www.facebook.com/groups/nomoreboxes

Step 2: Understanding - Get to Know the Box

Step 2 is all about getting to know and understand the Boxes around you.

You might ask the following questions...

Am I in a Gender Box?
And if so, what are the drivers that lead me here?
Who put me there?
Was it me, or someone else?

And after that, it would be great to explore...

Is it a Good, Bad or Ugly Box (or a mixture)?
How does it serve me?
How does it serve others?

What are the benefits and advantages?
Does it bring me happiness or joy?
If so, how?
How does it harm or limit me or others?

What are the disadvantages, limitations or issues around being in this Gender Box for me or for other people?

What would my life be like, look like or feel like if I didn't have those and what would the world look like?

We know they're big questions, but that's the power of understanding the Gender Box.

When you've done with that, you're ready to move on to **Step 3.**

Step 3: Action - Love, Leave or Live with Your Box

In this step you can make the final decision whether to love or like the Gender Box that you're potentially in. If it's not serving you as well as it could, how can you escape from the box, remembering that sometimes just realising that someone put you in a box is enough to liberate you!

Thank you for joining us on this wild, boxy journey, and if you've found this helpful, insightful and you know it will make a difference to the world, then we invite you to support the #NoMoreBoxes movement by becoming a Patron. To do that, head on over to www.patreon.com/nomoreboxes

Here's to human liberation, peace, happiness, and you

- and to **#NoMoreBadLimitingDivisiveUglyCruelUnkindBoxesButKeepTheRest**

About The Change Makers

The Change Makers are a group of international thought-leaders in the leadership and business world coming together to empower humans to be the change they want to see in their world. **The Change Makers** consist of CEO and founder, **Rúna Magnúsdóttir,** Kindness Ambassador and Five Institute CEO **Nicholas Haines**, Paradigm Shifter for High-Achievers **Gido Schimanski**, Creator of The Magnetic Leadership Program **Susanne Frandsen**, Kull Leadership founder **Margareta Kull**, visual director **Bjarney Ludviksdottir** and Business Launch Portal CEO **Monique Blokzyl**.

ACKNOWLEDGEMENTS

No woman or man is an island. Writing this book has been quite a journey for us, the authors. We could not have done it without tremendous love, support and help from people, who like us, want the world to be a place where everyone is respected, valued and free to be who they authentically are in a safe, kind and sustainable environment.

A big thank you to Leslie Grossman, one of our global advisory board members, for inviting us in the first place to attend the Impact Leadership Global Summit at the United Nations where the whole #NoMoreBoxes movement started. A warm thank you to all of The Change Makers, Gido Schimanski, Margareta Kull, Monique Blokzyl, Bjarney Ludviksdottir and Susanne Frandsen for all your endless support throughout the work of writing this book.

A massively big thank you to our proofreaders; Thoranna K. Jonsdottir , Emily Aristotelous and Olafur J. Straumland for lending us their amazing laser eyes, spotting all the little details that we no longer noticed in the copy. We feel so grateful for all the countless hours you have given us.

We would also like to express our deep gratitude to Kristin Arnadottir the Ambassador of Equality in Iceland for supporting us setting up our #NoMoreBoxes Breakfast Clubs in various Icelandic Embassies worldwide where we gathered local influencers, CEO's and politicians for open and honest conversations around gender, diversity and equality in such a way that it allows everyone to find and be part of the solution.

Finally, we would like to shine love and light to our partners in life, Sue and Oli who have had to listen to us rambling about boxes for most of this year. Thank you for your endless love, support and belief in our mission to create a world that is more inclusive, kind, sustainable and just.

Rúna & Nick

ABOUT RÚNA MAGNÚSDÓTTIR

(a.k.a. Rúna Magnús)

An internationally acclaimed personal branding speaker, author and strategist. Author of the book and awarded personal branding program; *Branding Your X-Factor, How the Secret to Your Success is Already Right In Front of Your....*

Founder and CEO The Change Makers co-creator of the #NoMoreBoxes Movement and Breakfast Club™

Born, raised and living in Iceland. Rúna is an globally active advocate for gender equity in the world. She is the past vice-president of FKA (The Icelandic Association of Women Business Leaders) and serves on several global advisory boards worldwide advocating for more gender diversity in leadership roles in the world.

As an international transformational teacher and a sought after international speaker, Rúna uses her lifetime experience as an entrepreneur, *her shaken but not stirred* sense of humour with a good dash of passion to speak, inspire and empower humans to be the change they want to see in their world.

www.RunaMagnus.com
www.NoMoreBoxesMovement.com

Twitter: @runamagnus
Instagram: @runamagnus
Facebook: @runamagnusOfficial

About Nicholas Haines

Nicholas Haines is a **Kindness Ambassador & Life Architect** and the creator of **The Vitality Test,** as well as an international speaker, author, strategist and teacher in Chinese Energetics.

He is the co-founder of the **Five Institute** and a founding member of The Change Makers and co-creator of the #NoMoreBoxes Movement and Breakfast Club™

In his role as a Kindness Ambassador at the Five Institute he is actively creating a world where Kindness is the common language and way of life. From how you treat yourself and others, to how families, business cultures, governments and international change operate.

Nick helped steer the provision of complementary therapies into one of the most deprived areas of the UK & helped the project win a prestigious government award for Integrated & Complementary healthcare.

Through his work at the **Five Institute,** which is the home of **The Vitality Test** and with **The Change Makers** Nick has been engaged by a diverse range of companies and organizations from leadership teams within large corporations through to NHS hospitals, educational institutes and international governments, where he addresses issues around relationships, cultures, communication, diversity, gender, empowerment and kindness.

www.Nicholas-Haines.com
www.FiveInstitute.com

Twitter: @nickhainesfive
Instagram: @nickhainesfive
Facebook: @nick.haines1

www.ingramcontent.com/pod-product-compliance
Lightning Source LLC
Chambersburg PA
CBHW021006160726
47994CB00006B/2392